Western Mexico
A Traveller's Treasury

Step inside...

Western Mexico
A Traveller's Treasury

Tony Burton

Illustrated by Mark Eager

P
P

PERCEPTION PRESS • SAINT AUGUSTINE, FLORIDA

To Marisa and Trevor

.

Distributed by **Gordon Soules Book
Publishers Ltd.** ● 1359 Ambleside Lane,
West Vancouver, BC, Canada V7T 2Y9
● PMB 620, 1916 Pike Place #12,
Seattle, WA 98101-1097 US
E-mail: books@gordonsoules.com
Web site: http://www.gordonsoules.com
(604) 922 6588 Fax: (604) 688 5442

Western Mexico – A Traveller's Treasury

ISBN 1-893518-01-9
Third edition 2001
(previously published by Editorial Agata, ISBN 968-7310-71-5)
Text and Maps © 1993, 1994, 1997, 1999 by Tony Burton
Illustrations © 1993 by Mark Eager
Design, maps and typography by Carol Wheeler Esparza

Published by Perception Press
Box 1855, Saint Augustine, Florida 32085-1855, U.S.A.
Inquiries in Canada: Box 4,   Ladysmith, BC   V9G 1A1, Canada

Printed in Canada

1

Contents

Illustrations

4

Acknowledgements

I owe an immense debt of gratitude to many people, without whose help this book would never have been written. Unfailing in his encouragement, Jorge Romo published early versions of several of the chapters in his monthly newspapers, the *Chapala Riviera Guide* (now *Magazine*) and the *Manzanillo Riviera Guide*. Some paragraphs used in chapters 6, 7, 18 and 29 were first published in *El Ojo del Lago*. Its publisher, Richard Tingen, has also been completely supportive of the present venture. Other parts of the book first appeared in *Travelmex*. My grateful thanks to all the editors involved for their assistance. Versions of some of this material later appeared in the *Jalisco State News,* with the author's permission, in a booklet about Lake Chapala and in a US-published retirement guide.

The editor of *Travelmex,* Carol Wheeler Esparza, kindly agreed to edit the text and is responsible for the layout. That walking encyclopaedia of all things Mexican, Carlos Meléndez, generously agreed to read the entire manuscript and made a large number of helpful corrections and suggestions. David Brown, Everett Minor, Phyllis Rauch, Hugh Robertson, and my mother all offered valuable advice. Last, but not least, my wife Gwen will be delighted to end her proof-reading, a task she performed with her customary good-humour and cheerfulness.

Needless to say, the errors which remain, whether of style or fact, are, regrettably, my own.

• • •

Introduction

B y the strictest definition, this is neither a travel-book nor a guide-book, but combines elements of both. It is certainly not meant to be a comprehensive guide to all the possible day trips and longer tours in the region; such a task would require an encyclopaedia. Neither is it a diary describing my fourteen years of living and travelling in Mexico. Rather, it is a personal, idiosyncratic collection of my favourite places in Western Mexico, places which I feel sure you, too, will enjoy.

Don't look here for details of Puerto Vallarta, Manzanillo, Guadalajara or Morelia. These large cities, which have brought millions of visitors to the region, are well described in conventional guidebooks. The present eclectic collection of suggested trips aims to provide everyone with something to enjoy once they venture beyond the cities. One or two hotels and a handful of restaurants have found their way into the text but only because they are themselves interesting or unique attractions.

All the places described offer a glimpse of the Mexico behind the mask, the hidden Mexico which does not offer herself up easily for sacrifice and dissection on the tourist equivalent of the Chac Mool. And this, of course, is the country's great charm. Far from the resorts, much of Mexico has retained her ancient culture and her ancient traditions.

A mixture of interests is represented. Here are historical places such as Lagos de Moreno and San Blas, artistic colonies such as Ajijic, lakeside communities like Chapala, ecological wonders including Manantlán and the monarch butterflies, coastal resorts such as Barra de Navidad, Indian villages like Angahuan, and a host of others....

All the destinations in parts one and two are within day-trip range (maximum three hours driving time), of Guadalajara or Chapala. For driving times from other cities, see Appendix. Obviously, it may be better to spend your time on any single trip exploring just one or two of the places mentioned.

In part three, all the locations described are worth at least an overnight stay, though Tapalpa, Mazamitla and Tamazula are still within three hours driving time of Guadalajara-Chapala. Parts four to eight describe longer, three or four day trips, all of which are well worth the investment of extra time.

The gaps between parts, as portrayed on the cover map, should not be taken to mean that there is nothing worth seeing there. This book will have succeeded even if it only whets your appetite to go exploring such areas – for then you will have the pleasure of discovering for yourself still more of Western Mexico's hidden treasures.

• • •

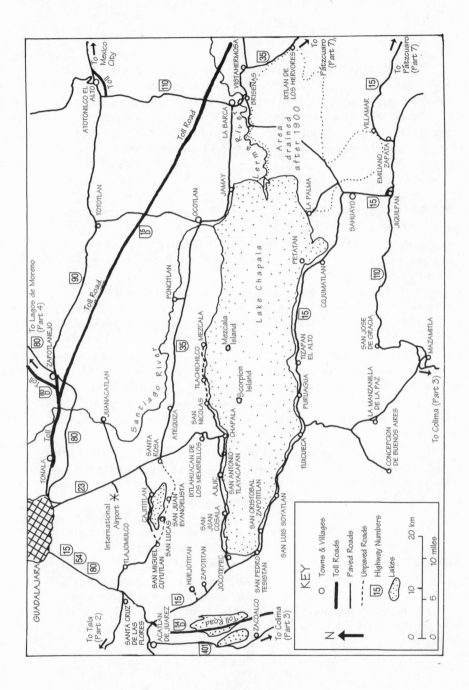

Part One

1. The Conquistadores Reach Chapala's Shores

The earliest human inhabitants of the Lake Chapala area were probably nomadic tribes of Indians who had eventually settled on the shores and islands of the lake, catching fish, perhaps extracting salt, and maybe trying to herd wild game towards the water's edge so that it would fall in and drown. In the Regional Museum in Guadalajara are the skeletons of numerous animals, including mammoths and early members of the horse family, which have been recovered from beneath the old lake bed.

Some historians have argued that the Aztecs may have settled temporarily on the shores of Lake Chapala and later on the shores of Lake Pátzcuaro during their long two-hundred year migration from their homeland, Aztlán, (see chapter 21), en route to founding their capital city, Tenochtitlan, where Mexico City stands today.

By the time the Spanish arrived, one particular tribe, the Cocas, had settled on the northern lakeshore, in Cutzalán (today called San Juan Cosalá).

The Cocas' main god was Ixtlacateotl who presided over their dancing and drinking fiestas and was offered the hearts of captives taken during battle. The Cocas spent much of their time fighting off repeated advances of the Tarascan Indians from the Lake Pátzcuaro area to the east. To prepare themselves for battle, the Cocas showered themselves with their previous victims' blood believing that this would make them invincible in the coming struggle.

They also offered large numbers of ceramic pots and small jars, sprinkled or bathed in victims' blood, to their god, by throwing them into the lake. These "blood cups", as archaeologists call them, are still often recovered by local fishermen in their nets.

The northern slopes of Lake Chapala's basin were formerly wooded and the small Indian villages of pre-Columbian times had little impact on the local environment but the Cocas had a rapidly expanding population and in the mid-fourteenth century, their chief approved the founding of new villages at Axixic, (now Ajijic), Xilotepec, (now Jocotepec), Tzapotitlán (now San Cristobal Zapotitlán) and Tomatlán (an unknown location).

When the Spanish arrived in late 1523 or early 1524, their leader, Captain Alonso de Avalos, a cousin of Hernán Cortés, was, according to Spanish accounts, able to persuade the Cocas to give up without a fight. Later, the Coca chief, Xitomatl (or Tzacuaco) was baptised Andrés Carlos and the Franciscan priests who had originally chosen St. Francis as patron saint of Axixic ("place where the water splashes"), decided that it was more fitting to bestow the name of San Andrés on the church there. The church had been finished in 1539.

The Spanish moved the settlement of Xilotepec ("place of the tender corn")

How the Lake was Formed

L ake Chapala is Mexico's largest natural lake. On the geological timescale of millions of years, all lakes are temporary features on the earth's surface. Once formed, natural processes begin to fill them in and/or to drain them.

Lake Chapala resulted from drastic earth movements, accompanied by earthquakes and faulting which occurred some twelve million years ago. Given its advanced age, it is not surprising to discover that it was once (we're now talking thousands of years) much larger. In fact, though no one has so far proven it beyond doubt, it may have been immensely large, covering an area seven times its present size, with a correspondingly enormous shoreline. At a later stage in its history, Chapala was the deepest of an interconnected series of lakes which flooded the valley floors where the towns of Jocotepec, Zapotitán, Zacoalco and Sayula are today.

The present Lake Chapala is thus only a small remnant of the original version and under heavier pressure than at any time in its existence. Local towns and the nearby city of Guadalajara regard it as an inexhaustible supply of domestic and industrial water. Tourists see it as a recreation resource, and foreign retirees as a major reason for the area's beneficial climate. The levels of flow in the entering Lerma river are crucial to the health of the lake. In recent years, demands for Lerma water have multiplied many times over, principally for farms in neighbouring states, but also for industries. All the other rivers entering the lake are much smaller and with rare exception flow into the lake only a few times a year, during the rainy season.

• • •

and renamed it San Francisco Xocotepec, ("place of the guavas") which in time became simply Jocotepec. The official refounding was on 20th November, 1529. Guavas are a native fruit (*Psidium guajava*) with a characteristic slightly acid flavour and a musky penetrating smell. In recent years, Jocotepec, "the place of the fruit", has become much better known for its raspberries, exported to Europe, the USA and Canada, than for its guavas.

There are almost as many possible explanations for the name "Chapala" as there are historians who have tried to explain it. It may derive from "Chapatla" which in turn came from "Chapatlán" or "Chachapatlán", meaning "place where there are many pots", a possible reference to the blood-cups mentioned earlier. It may, on the other hand, be named for an Indian chief Chapa who lived in the area when the Franciscans arrived. Another possibility is from "Chapalac", marshy or wet place; yet another is from "Chapalal", supposed to represent the sound made by waves splashing onto a beach. Whatever the derivation, the word Chapala came to be used not only for the lake but also for the most important tourist town on its shores, first founded as long ago as 1510.

• • •

The fortress on Mezcala island

2. The Island of Mezcala
Lake Chapala's National Monument

On a small island in the middle of Lake Chapala stand the ruins of a fortress which was the scene of a glorious episode in Mexican history. Between 1812 and 1816, a determined band of insurgents repeatedly repelled the best efforts of the much more powerful and better armed Royalist army and navy to dislodge them from their island stronghold.

The fate of the group of desperados on Mezcala island echoed events in the country as a whole and their four year struggle against the odds remains one of the most abiding and extraordinary chapters written on Mexico's long road to independence from Spain, finally achieved in 1821.

The protagonists on the rebel side were a mixed bunch. Encarnación Rosas, probably born in Chapala, had been sickened by the Crown troops' barbaric butchering of ordinary civilians. Marcos Castellanos was a priest who had officiated in Sahuayo and Ocotlán. Luis Macías was owner of the hacienda La Palma. José Santana was a local Indian from Mezcala village. Perhaps more than anything else, this motley crew serves to demonstrate the futility of claiming that Mexican independence was simply the end result of class inequalities, for here was a humble Indian alongside a rich land owner, and a creole priest, alongside a *mestizo* out for revenge.

In October 1812, after a series of battles on the northern shore and facing overwhelming odds, the rebels decided to retreat to Mezcala island. The ruined buildings seen today on the island are of uncertain age. They probably predate independence but have been substantially modified since. The rebels strengthened their island fortress by driving pointed stakes into the lake bed, leaving their sharpened tips submerged beneath the water line. They built ramparts, storehouses, and a small chapel for their religious well-being. For the next four years the island was the home of up to 1000 men at a time, plus women and children.

The first efforts to dislodge the insurgents were made by Angel Linares. In Tizapán el Alto, he killed a few suspected collaborators of the rebels, including Rosas' wife. In February1813, Linares attacked the island with several big boats

View from Mezcala Island

brought over the mountains all the way from San Blas on the Pacific coast.

Insurgent spies forewarned the men on the island, who set sail in their canoes. In the ensuing debacle, two Royalist canoes were sunk and Linares was captured. The only Royalist canoes to escape were those which arrived late.

The Royalist Commander General, José de la Cruz, was furious and placed Pedro Negrete and 1200 men in Tlachichilco, a small village opposite the island. He also demanded more boats from San Blas, together with sailors and artillery.

The insurgents busied themselves reprovisioning the island and making more bullets. They installed more cannons and built more stone walls. They also launched lightning-quick attacks on first one and then another lakeside village. One day it might be Ocotlán, the next Jamay, then Tizapán, then Jocotepec....

In June 1813, Negrete attacked, but only after having first sent an emissary with a white flag requesting the rebels' surrender. The insurgents' reply, roughly translated, was "No! Let blood run first!"

Negrete's men attacked but were brutally repelled by cannon-balls and stones.

Aided by a following wind, they tried again. This time they reached the underwater stakes and stones which protected the island, but their biggest boat, the "San Fernando", ran aground. Those Royalists who made it to the beach were slaughtered. Negrete himself lost two fingers from his left hand in the desperate fighting and resigned his command.

Negrete's replacement, José Navarro, changed strategy. He proposed to blockade the island until the rebels ran out of food and ammunition. In July 1813, all local hacienda owners were ordered to desist from supplying the island, or suffer the consequences. But the wily insurgents raided Ajijic and Tizapán el Alto for fresh food, timber and weapons. The Royalists evacuated their wounded to Guadalajara at night, so that news of their defeat would not be too widely publicised.

For the remainder of 1814 and most of 1815, the Mezcala defenders enjoyed themselves, overturning Royalist canoes and sneaking in more supplies. They continued to harass the Royalist forces occupying the lakeside villages. Sometime during this period, Castellanos decided to systematically burn all rebel-held documents, to the immense frustration of later historians. At one point, Navarro cleared the south coast of Chapala of all livestock but the insurgents still refused to surrender.

José Santana was involved in much of the action. On May 25th, he attacked Jocotepec and was forced to hide in the church before making good his escape. The next day he led an attack on a select force of dragoons, capturing arms and food. But his luck finally ran out. After attacking Atequiza, Santana was surprised by a strong Royalist force and lost 300 men and four cannons, though at least he himself escaped to tell the tale.

De la Cruz, the Royalist General, had several times offered a pardon to the rebels, who had always refused to consider it. Now, as the winter of 1816 approached, conditions on the island were worsening. The rebels' water problems were acute and unsanitary conditions on the island had resulted in an epidemic of dysentery or typhoid, decimating their fighting strength. Santana, their leader, went to Tlachichilco to bargain with de la Cruz.

The General, with no way of knowing for sure how bad the rebels' situation was but with thousands of his men deployed in time-consuming and futile attempts to regain control of the island, was more than ready to listen to Santana. Santana bargained for the rebels to be given a full pardon, for their villages to be rebuilt, for seeds and animals to be provided, for Father Castellanos to be given a good curacy, and for baptisms, weddings and burials to be free of tax. To Santana's amazement, de la Cruz agreed immediately.

On the afternoon of the 25th of November, 1816, de la Cruz formally took possession of the island and the insurgents returned to their mainland villages. De la Cruz kept his word and Castellanos became priest of Ajijic.

The insurgents' brave resistance to colonial rule inspired others and, before the end of 1821, Mexico had become independent, closing forever the 300-year-long chapter of colonialism.

Within months of their "success", the Royalists decided that the island was

The Famous Chapala Whitefish

E ver since tourism began in the Chapala region, the lake's whitefish has been considered a highly desirable local delicacy. At the turn of the century, Tweedie wrote "Delicious fish abound in the Lake, which is about eighty miles long; they are caught in nets. These *pescado blanco* (white fish) are literally transparent when they come out of the water. They are spoken of as lake herring, though I cannot say I thought they resembled a Loch Fyne herring in taste so much as a river trout".

The whitefish is not really a single species of fish, but one of several members of the *Chirostoma* genus, and is identical to the Lake Pátzcuaro whitefish.

Production of white fish in Lake Chapala peaked in the 1940's, reaching a maximum of 149 metric tons in 1946. The steady decline since then has been due to the increased pollution of the lake, aggravated by varying lake levels, overfishing, the introduction of aggressive carp (*Cyprinus*) which eats the eggs and young fish of other species, and in some parts of the lake, the fishing techniques employed.

The fame of the whitefish certainly spread far afield, and a wonderful anecdote is given about the notoriously difficult to transport delicacy in Clark (1944):

"A popular story relates that President Díaz once sent a tankful of live *pescados blancos* to King Edward VII and Edward liked them so very much, and said so, that the Mexican dictator felt obliged to send him a fresh tankful each year. It was so extraordinarily difficult to achieve this with success that it caused something like an annual crisis in Mexican foreign policy, but perhaps it did at least offer a practical and interesting problem to the dictator's *Científicos*. I did not blame King Edward when I sampled this fish...."

Nowadays, whitefish is but rarely found on the menus in most local restaurants and is very expensive. There is an on-going project centred on the area around Tizapán el Alto, on the south side of the lake, to restock the lake with whitefish.

• • •

best turned into a jail, presumably on the basis that this would effectively dis-
courage anyone from attempting to follow the insurgents' example. Two hundred
inmates were housed on Mezcala, in open-prison conditions, with workshops and
farms. The jail was run on a budget of fourteen hundred pesos a month.

In 1821, there were calls for Castellanos to be officially honoured but
Mexico's new leaders refused. A few years later, Count Baltrini, an Italian
traveller, found Castellanos as vehemently opposed to European exploitation as
ever. Castellanos died in February 1826 and was buried, a pauper, in Jocotepec.
Streets are named after him in several Jalisco towns, including Ajijic and
Guadalajara.

The Island Now

A visit to the ruins on Mezcala island, or Presidio Island, as some locals call
it, should be considered a "must" by any visitor to the area. The cobblestone paths,
crumbling walls, ancient doorways, and glorious views from the island, views
which serve as reminders of the ease with which a fortress here could control much
of the shoreline, all evoke those magical moments from early in the nineteenth
century when this valiant band of freedom fighters withstood the might of Spain.
At the time, events on Mezcala perhaps seemed to have only local or regional
significance; with the hindsight afforded by history, they assume truly national
importance.

Of all the buildings remaining from this turbulent period of Mexican history,
those which have survived on Mezcala are unique – they are the only ones known
which were built or converted by a group of insurgents, and from which they were
never displaced by force of arms.

Mezcala Village

From Mezcala village, on the mainland, there is an interesting walk for the
more adventurous to the base of the steep hills north east of the village school. A
wide vehicle track which soon becomes only a horse-trail leads past stony fields
of maize and out onto a pile of loose rocks at the entrance to a narrow, high and
precipitously-sided cleft in the mountain side. This veritable gorge formed millenia ago along the line of a geological fault was further deepened by a torrential
deluge of rain in the 1970's. It has a mysterious and slightly eerie atmosphere and
is a fascinating place to explore and to look for strange plant and insect life.

The area around Mezcala is one of the best bird-watching locations anywhere
along the Lake Chapala shoreline. Where the wooded slopes behind the village
merge into the small cultivated plots of maize and vegetables on the flatter land,
it is common to spot colourful hooded orioles, and down on the lakeshore, look
not only for waterbirds such as great and snowy egrets, but also for the spectacular
flycatchers such as the vermilion flycatcher and the great kiskadee. From out on
the island, white pelicans are seen most winters and the island itself is home to a
large number of black-crowned night herons and groove-billed anis, both of which

make for interesting viewing.

A walk around the village and a visit to the island fortress can easily be combined into a single day out, but be sure to take a picnic lunch since the village of Mezcala lacks a restaurant or any tourist facilities.

To Get There

From the town of Chapala, the boat-ride to the island takes about 50 minutes each way. Boats seat eight to ten people and the cost should be negotiated before leaving the pier. Allow 90 minutes to explore the island. From Mezcala village local fishermen make the trip to the island in about twenty minutes.

Driving to Mezcala village (thirty minutes east of Chapala past San Nicolás, on a dirt road) is made even more worthwhile by its scenery. With views encompassing small, private bays, steep cliffs and luxuriant green vegetation down to the water's edge, this is a totally unspoilt and undiscovered section of the northern lakeshore.

• • •

3. Tourism takes off in Chapala

T he splendid old Chapala railway station building, on the edge of the Las Redes subdivision, is set to become another major tourist attraction in Chapala, once it has been restored and refurbished as a museum or cultural centre. This building, donated to the State Government by the González Gallo family, is one of the oldest and most interesting buildings in Chapala.

The origins of Chapala tourism, and the background to the railway, go back to the mid nineteenth century when a single guest-house, that of Doña Trini, existed in the town. In 1868, the machinery for a steamboat was brought from California by sea to San Blas and then over the mountains on burros to Chapala. Later that year the "Libertad" (Freedom) was launched on the lake.

In 1889, on March 24th, this boat sank while approaching Ocotlán at the eastern end of the lake, killing more than 50 passengers. It is said that the sinking occurred because merrymaking passengers, returning from a fiesta, all rushed simultaneously to the same side of the boat as it approached the shore, causing it to capsize. "The boiler lies on the beach, a rusty monument to American pluck and energy." (Campbell, 1899)

The "Libertad", minus its boiler, was refloated in 1890 and renamed the "Ramón Corona", in honour of the Jalisco state governor assassinated the previous year (page 37). Later, the"Ramón Corona" was transferred to Lake Pátzcuaro.

Besides the steamboats, sail boats plied the waters of the lake, ferrying passengers and their goods from one small fishing village to another. These vessels had a distinctive Asiatic look to them. Models of them can be seen today in the Chapala Haciendas hotel and the Ocotlán museum.

Even before the turn of the century, proposals had been made for a rail link from Guadalajara to Chapala, though these early proposals all came to nothing. Mexican National Railways, however, began to offer trips by train to Ocotlán, with connecting service to the town of Chapala by lake steamer. The boats,

Chapala railway station

"Carmelita" and "Fritz", made daily runs, leaving at 9:00 a.m., returning at 4:00 p.m. Some visitors preferred taking the train only as far as Atequiza, followed by a three hour horseback ride into Chapala. Another alternative was to go all the way by horse or stage-coach, but this involved a change of horses near the present-day airport, and was a tough 12-hour trip, usually necessitating an overnight stop.

Rail was very much the preferred way to travel in those days and the trip from Guadalajara to either Atequiza or Ocotlán passed one of Mexico's most impressive natural sights, the waterfalls of Juanacatlán (page 50).

In 1895 Septimus Crow (perhaps Crowe) arrived. *Don* Septimus was probably English, and he fell in love with the lake, the local people, and Chapala's thermal baths. He bought land and built a house where the Montecarlo Hotel is today. Then he bought more land and built the Villa Bell, and later the Villa Josefina. Crow was the area's first real-estate developer, and was personally responsible for persuading many of his friends to settle in Chapala, beginning the influx of non-Mexican residents. He died in 1903. He is perhaps best remembered today for having had a street named after him – the "Callejón de Mister Crow" – one block east of the Montecarlo Hotel, very close to where the flow of thermal water under the highway causes the road surface to buckle and tilt.

Near the end of the century, the English Consul in Mexico, Lionel Garden, was attracted to the lake and built a ranch, "Tlalocán", which was later owned by Manuel Cuesta Gallardo, who built a summer house there for President Porfirio Díaz. Díaz never occupied this building, since the Mexican Revolution broke out (in 1910) before he had chance. Cuesta Gallardo obtained permission from President Díaz to reclaim more than 50,000 hectares (120,000 acres) of lakebed at the eastern end of the lake for agriculture – building an eighty kilometre (fifty mile) long earth bank to protect it.

In 1898, Ignacio Arzapalo opened the Hotel Arzapalo in Chapala and began a daily stage-coach service to Atequiza, the nearest railway station. This proved to be a great success and, in 1905, on the site where the Hotel Nido now stands, Arzapalo began to build the two-storey, 96-room Hotel Palmera.

President Díaz, who had been President of Mexico, except for a brief three year period ever since 1877, visited Chapala in 1904, and for a week each Easter for several years thereafter. He stayed in El Manglar, owned by Lorenzo Elizaga. Cocktails called *chatos* (christened after Elizaga's nickname, "El Chato") were served, and the State Band would be sent from Guadalajara to provide entertainment. Díaz's last visit to Chapala was in 1909.

The popularity of Chapala grew. The Presidential seal of approval encouraged many noted Guadalajara families, such as Uribe, Pérez Verdía, Hermosillo, Capetillo, Castellanos, Somellera, Brizuela and Newton, to build or purchase houses on the lake. In 1906, a very distinctive, European-style house built by historian Luis Pérez Verdía was sold to one Alberto Braniff, from Mexico City.

Braniff was a member of the famous airline family, and spent up to a month each year in Chapala. He introduced many sports into Chapala, including bullfighting, and brought motorboats to the lake. His brother, Tomás, had the area's best sailboats. The Braniff family sold their house in 1942. It is a restaurant, the Cazadores, today.

To Chapala by Stagecoach in 1901

T he English gentlelady, Mrs. Alec Tweedie, visited Mexico in 1901. In her eight months of wanderings, she slept in sixty-two different beds: "A Mexican bed also has its little peculiarity; it may be of brass, of iron, or wood, but the mattress – judging by its hardness – is of the same substance as the frame".

To reach Chapala's "famous waters", she took the train as far as Atequiza before changing to a ten-passenger stage-coach or diligence. "It was exactly a Lord Mayor's coach, although adorned with scarlet and gold...its eight mules, though almost small enough for mice, possessed the strength of those lions who still wander at large in Mexico."

"...before us sat the driver holding six reins and a whip, his feet resting upon the brake; next to him was his "help" with two whips... the first was short... the second whip was some twenty-four feet long with a short handle... it is said no white man can ever ride, drive, or pack a mule properly!"

"It was a glorious drive through the mountains to Chapala Lake. We galloped most of the way, bumped over bad roads and swung round corners... the sun shone brilliantly... Every now and then something went wrong with the brake; down jumped the help, ... he hacked the old one off, and then proceeded to tie the new one on. No coach in Mexico ever proceeds far on a journey ere requiring some repairs of this sort, and the "helps" are wonderfully clever in arranging such trifles. "Done," he called, and off the driver started, leaving the poor help hanging like a fly to the step..."

"The heavy old coach, hanging on thick leather straps, swung from side to side; boulders on the road, rivers across the path and such trifles nearly sent us flying from our seats... but nothing really happened, it was all in the day's work.... Eagles and hawks flew overhead, and in the distance we saw Colima, one of the few active volcanoes in Mexico, some ninety miles away, and only about sixty miles distant from the Pacific Coast."

(Tweedie, 1901.)

• • •

In 1908, a Norwegian entrepreneur, Christian Schjetnan, visited Chapala from the U.S.A. He was much taken with the area, and on his return to the States, he formed a tourist development company which included Porfirio Díaz, Limantour and Lorenzo Elizaga. The Company began operations in 1909, importing into Mexico a prefabricated wooden yacht club building. This was assembled on metal posts about 150 yards from the pier. It was a one-storey building with offices, a library, dance room, restaurant, terraces, a lookout and a lighthouse, which never worked. Absolutely everything was imported from the U.S. – the furniture, the cutlery and even the tablecloths. The club also imported three sail boats, none of which survived long. The "Condor", about sixty feet long, was eventually abandoned in Ajijic, and the "Oslo" and the "Urca" both ran aground on Scorpion Island.

The clubhouse was inaugurated early in April of 1910, but given the signs of the impending Revolution then obvious in the country, the opening was not well attended, especially since President Díaz, soon to be deposed, was one of the principal share-holders. On December 27th 1911, the club was reinaugurated, much more spectacularly, with regattas, parties and firework displays.

The Mexican Revolution continued, and in 1914 the yacht club was abandoned. It became open-access, and locals held their parties there. In 1917, it was burnt down. According to local lore, a young Chapala boy, thwarted in love, was walking past the building when he decided to make a fresh start. He set fire to his former love's letters and threw them over his shoulder... Unfortunately, the burning papers landed in the wooden yacht club....

But Norwegians are tenacious people, and Schjetnan, undeterred by the failure of the yacht club, carried on. In 1918 he began plans to launch two new steam-boats on the lake – the "Vicking", with two decks, for passengers, and the "Tapatío" for freight – and to construct a private railway line from Chapala to the Mexican National Railway at La Capilla near Atequiza.

The railway station, one of the most beautiful stations ever constructed in Mexico, finally opened in 1920, with twice daily service. The oft-repeated claim that former Mexican President, Porfirio Díaz, was a frequent user of the railway station, however appealing, is thus without foundation – unless he did so post-humously – since Díaz had died in 1915! Sadly, the railway quickly ran into problems. In 1926 the lake rose by more than a metre and flooded the picturesque station, built right on the beach. Later that same year, the "Vicking" was battered and destroyed by storm waves, and then the railway ceased operation.

Alternative modes of land-based transport, especially the new motor-car and motor-buses, proved to be both more efficient and cheaper. The first motor-car to reach Chapala was "Protos", which arrived at 11:55 a.m. on December 31st, 1909, driven by Benjamin Hurtado. By 1917, solid-tyre autobuses for 40 passengers were being operated by Garnot and Maldonat of Guadalajara. The bus trip to the lake took about five hours each way.

The closing of the railway station brought to an end a marvellous chapter in the dreams of the early twentieth century entrepreneurs and pioneers who raised the sleepy town of Chapala to national prominence. Their efforts initiated the influx of foreign residents which has continued to the present day.

What more fitting monument to Chapala's history and changing fortunes could there be than a museum of local history housed in this lovely building?

• • •

4. The Riviera Communities
Chapala, Ajijic and Jocotepec

Chapala – Something for everyone.

"C hapala enjoys a glorious climate, tropical vegetation abounds, and birds and beasts from every clime shelter along the shores of the lake... In the evening we went out to look at the moon on Chapala lake – one of those lovely moons all lakes know so well how to reflect... What a lovely evening that was at Chapala...." (Tweedie, 1901)

Besides the attractions of its climate, scenery and the moonlight on the lake, Chapala today offers a wide range of tourist facilities including more sports facilities than any other lakeside town.

But you don't have to be an active or sports-minded person to enjoy Chapala. There are numerous restaurants, open-air cafes and ice-cream parlours in which to while away the siesta-time. A walk around the town can include visiting the parish church, San Francisco, which whilst not particularly old, has a literary distinction, having been immortalised by D. H. Lawrence in the last pages of his novel, *The Plumed Serpent,* written during Lawrence's brief stay in Chapala at number 307 Zaragoza street.

It is also worth stepping inside the dining room of the Nido Hotel to look at their collection of old photographs of Chapala. These include some thought-provoking pictures of when the lake threatened to overwhelm the town; for a few weeks people preferred canoes to bicycles!

Chapala was officially refounded by the Spanish in 1538. On the Cerro San Miguel, the steep-sided hill west of the town, the first Spanish clerics in this area built a hermitage. Today a white cross is located there, a cross which is said to have stood for years on the exact site of the first Mass which was held down on the lakeshore. Only in 1924, when a street was resurfaced, was the cross moved to its

Lake Chapala

present location.

Cerro San Miguel is an obvious landmark often used by boats on the lake; it is clearly visible from virtually anywhere on the southern shoreline. Unfortunately, climbing the hill does not afford much of a view, since the vegetation has been allowed to grow too high. A much better view can be obtained from the hillsides further east. Vehicular access here is easy along a cobblestone road which leaves the main highway before Ixtlahuacán de los Membrillos, about five kilometres north of Chapala. The large quarry on this road has unusual basaltic prisms.

At weekends, the liveliest place from which to watch the world go by is the Beergarden, an institution in Chapala for more than 60 years, where, on Sunday afternoons, competing mariachi musicians strive to outdo each other in claiming your attention.

If you don't have your own boat, then Chapala pier is the place to contract a local launch. The boatmen, competing fiercely with each other, will try to convince you of the delights of visiting Scorpion Island and its restaurants. Just make sure you agree on the price beforehand.

If you do have your own boat, you will want to walk from the pier, past the well-kept lakeshore gardens and a small children's park, and visit the Chapala yacht club, which has by far the best storage and launching facilities on the lake. The club, which has by far the best storage and launching facilities on the lake. The clubhouse is an attractive building, often used for art exhibitions and cocktail parties.

Not surprisingly, the row of small restaurants next to the yacht club all specialise in fish. At weekends, this area, like the Beergarden, is a cacophony of mariachi sound. Nearby, the Chapala handicrafts market provides an excellent place to shop for inexpensive gifts. The vendors have a very wide range of tempting bargains on display ranging from leather jackets, wooden furniture, and hand-embroidered dresses to decorated glassware, ceramics and trinkets.

Two minutes walk from the handicrafts market is the Christiania park. Excluding parks in large cities, this is one of the finest public sporting installations in the country. A very modest entrance fee gives access to a well-equipped children's playground, snack-bar, and huge, grassed and scrupulously-clean picnic area. Additional charges are levied on users of the park's tennis courts and monster swimming pool. The Christiania park undoubtedly represents one of the great bargains in Mexico.

More expensive but still good value is a game of golf. The Chapala Country Club, whose course was once on the same property where the park is today, now has an excellent nine-hole course on the slopes overlooking the lake near San Nicolás, ten minutes drive east of Chapala. The club is open to non-members on payment of a green fee. The course makes imaginative use of alternative tees, front nine and back nine, to give it the character of a regulation par-72, 18-hole course. The clubhouse, where ample drinks and excellent food await, is a pleasant place to relax after your game.

There is another golf course on the way to Ajijic, the Chula Vista Country Club. This course may not be very long, but is certainly very tricky. Its nine holes, totalling only 1800 metres, are made up of five par threes and four par fours, requiring great accuracy for a good score. From most parts of the course, which is surrounded by beautiful private homes, there is a panoramic view over Ajijic and San Antonio.

If all these sports facilities only serve to make your muscles ache, then the best place to go is the Montecarlo hotel. This private club and hotel, which has extensive gardens sloping down to the lake, is open to day-visitors on payment of an entrance fee. One of its swimming pools has unusually warm thermal water with a reputation for curative properties. Lying in this hot, circular pool is an ideal way to ease away those aches and pains caused by too much, or too little, exercise.

Ajijic and San Antonio – Arts, Crafts and Culture

Since the 1950's, Ajijic has been considered the artistic centre of the Chapala Riviera. Its artistic colony is comprised of both Mexicans and non-Mexicans, working in a variety of media. Almost always, there are several current exhibitions open to the public, either in local galleries and stores, or in the hotels and restaurants. Often, an exhibiting artist is prepared to undertake a commission on

The Posada Ajijic

Over the years, the Posada Ajijic has seen it all. Hundreds of celebrities from every walk of life have eaten meals there or stayed in its simply furnished rooms, when it was an hotel as well as a restaurant-bar. Film stars, directors, writers, artists, producers, lawyers, politicians, athletes..., they all enjoyed it. Elizabeth Taylor, Charles Bronson, Dr. Marcus Welby, J.R. (as in *Dallas*) and his wife, the list is endless... Many of the Posada's clients returned year after year; one, Dr. Jim Vaughan, stayed there every year for the 35 years he visited Ajijic. Another, Kate Wolfe, a concert pianist, always stayed in room 11. One guest stayed in the hotel for two and a half years.

The Posada food gained such a reputation that one impoverished Ajijic hostess, striving to preserve the social graces even though she was in no financial position to do so, collected all the left-overs from her friends' meals in the restaurant to serve them again, suitably disguised, at her weekly "Bloody Mary" party.

• • •

request from a new buyer. Local newspapers and bulletin boards are the best sources of information about current shows and other events in the village.

The Ajijic stores offer a selection of Mexican handicrafts, household items, fashions and gifts, covering the entire economic range. Surprisingly, it is some- times difficult to encounter items actually made in the village – the larger local factories manufacture for export or wholesale only. On the other hand, several stores sell the choicest items from far-away Chiapas and Guatemala. One of the attractions of shopping in Ajijic is undoubtedly the personal attention that buyers receive, since many of the shop-assistants turn out to be the shop-owners, anxious to guarantee the best possible customer satisfaction.

Ajijic is a tourist-oriented oasis; probably no other similarly-sized village anywhere in Mexico has so many hotels, restaurants, bars and shops. There is accommodation to suit any budget: a trailer park, one-bedroom, fully equipped suites with kitchenettes, excellent bed-and-breakfast establishments with truly personal service, and a range of hotels including the luxury Real de Chapala and the unashamedly elegant Nueva Posada. From the lakeside garden restaurants of these two hotels, and from the restaurant-bar Posada Ajijic, you can eat, drink and enjoy the view across the lake, all at the same time.

The Posada Ajijic was established in the 1930's by Nigel Millet, an Englishman who, in collaboration with Peter Lilley, wrote *Village in the Sun,* a lively, thoughtful and incisive account of Ajijic life at the time. Sadly, this magnum opus of the local scene has long been out of print.

A handful of truly old buildings grace the village, including the parish church of San Andrés dating from 1749, the chapel of the Virgin of Santiago on the north side of the plaza, which is even older, and a former monastery at Hidalgo and Cinco de Mayo streets, which is now a luxurious private dwelling.

The fiesta in honour of San Andrés lasts for nine nights at the end of November (beginning and ending on a weekend) and has all the usual fairground amusements accompanied by music, folkloric dancing, and plenty of fireworks. There are daily processions in the streets and solemn masses for the devout. The Ajijic Easter celebration is gaining fame as one of the most extravagant in the country. Witnessed by the entire village, local farmers, fishermen, factory workers and tradespeople become actors for three days and re-enact the trial and crucifixion of Christ. The costuming and open-air sets are magnificent and this is a real "must be seen to be believed" occasion.

The neighbouring village of San Antonio still holds traditional *posadas,* dramatising Joseph and Mary's search for lodgings, on each of the nine nights before Christmas. Mary, seated on a donkey, is led through the streets. A children's choir accompanies her and formally requests lodgings at pre-arranged houses in the village, requests just as formally denied. The ever-growing procession ends up at the church where a mass is held, followed by a party with *piñatas* for the children.

First-time visitors to Ajijic often wonder why so many non-Mexicans have chosen to retire here. They are sometimes critical of the modern housing subdivisions on the outer edges of the village, perhaps failing to realise that many of the best houses really are "behind the walls". The house-and-garden tours, which are run weekly from December to March, are an excellent way to see much more than the casual visitor can normally hope to do in a short time. The proceeds of these tours, as of so many Ajijic events, benefit local charities, a fine example of how foreign retirees have made immense contributions to help repay the Lake Chapala riviera for its outstandingly favourable climate and the welcoming warmth of its inhabitants.

One of the modern subdivisions of Ajijic is named "Rancho del Oro" (Ranch of Gold). But "gold" is not just an idle reference to the sunshine which bathes Ajijic some 300 days a year – there really is gold, real gold, in the hills behind this sub-division. The small mining operations were abandoned as not being sufficiently profitable but what's to stop you from dreaming of instant wealth? – just bring your own gold pan.

If you prefer using a pan to cook rather than to find gold, then a fun way to try for instant success is to enter the annual Chili Cook-off, held in the village in February. This event, the winner of which carries off a fine trophy, several thousand dollars and an automatic place in the World Championships, is a three-day extravaganza with live entertainment and plenty of food (not just chili). Texan

Old Chapel, Ajijic

entrants beware – the competition rules state that no beans are allowed.

The sports minded visitor can also hike, play tennis, or ride horseback into the hills. There are any number of leisure-oriented clubs in Ajijic, most of which welcome visitors to their regular meetings, so whether you fancy a hand of bridge, meeting like-minded people, a Saturday morning walk with the Hash House Harriers, an English-language theatre production or a lesson in Tai Chi, simply check the listings in local newspapers and bulletin boards. There's always something to do in Ajijic.

San Juan Cosalá Spa

Lakeside's most popular spa is the Balneario San Juan, located mid-way between Ajijic and Jocotepec, in San Juan Cosalá, a small village founded hundreds of years before the Spanish arrived. It is best to visit the spa, which has excellent thermal pools, during the week, since on weekends or holidays it can be very crowded. The spa pools, together with a natural geyser, are next to the beach and provide an ideal way to ease away accumulated tensions. Massages can be booked and there is a restaurant.

Guests staying in the nearby Villas Buenaventura not only have thermal pools in their suites, but can also admire a fine collection of sculptures on display in the gardens. The sculptures were created during an International Sculpture Symposium held in the village in 1991.

Jocotepec – Where Traditions Thrive

The least touristy town along the northern lakeshore, Jocotepec, has a distinctive charm all of its own. Superficially, it has little to interest the visitor and only limited hotel and restaurant facilities. However, the town and local area have plenty to interest the more discerning traveller who delves beneath the surface.

The large central plaza which lies in the shadow of the towering hills is as attractive as any in the Riviera. It has a central bandstand and several monuments, including one in celebration of the 500th anniversary of Columbus' first voyage, and a stone disc, engraved with the town's coat-of-arms, erected to commemorate the 450th anniversary of the official founding of the town in 1529.

On Sunday evenings, the plaza is transformed into a scene of intense social activity as the townspeople gather to participate in the weekly *paseo*, in which young ladies, elegantly attired, walk clockwise around the central bandstand, whilst young men walk in the opposite direction. When a young man sees a young lady who interests him, he will give her a flower as she passes. Next time around, she may choose to sit out with her admirer on one of the many wrought-iron seats in the plaza thoughtfully provided for the purpose. Her elder sister or another family member will probably accompany her as chaperone but who knows what may result....

Under the arcades on two sides of the plaza small restaurants serve steaming plates of spicy *birria*, a kind of goat or mutton stew. People from far afield make long detours to ensure they don't miss sampling Jocotepec's birria at lunchtime, washed down with a beer or *refresco*.

People also come a long way to find the town's *curanderos,* experts in the art (or is it science?) of herbal medicine. For that matter, some come in search of the local *brujas* (witches), but that's another story....

No visit to Jocotepec is complete without a look inside the local churches. The large parish church of San Francisco looks benevolently over the plaza; being the main church in the town, you have a good chance of witnessing a first communion, baptism or marriage ceremony here. Nobody seems very sure just how old the building is. An original sixteenth century building on the site was destroyed by storm; its replacement, much modified since, probably dates from two hundred years later. The origin of the much venerated representation of Christ on the Cross is also unclear, though there are many alternative versions to choose from. One popular version claims that, way back in the sixteenth century, a local Indian was amazed on suddenly seeing a *guaje* tree (*Leucaena esculenta*) glow; he and a fishermen friend carved two sculptures out of the branches, one of which was the statue in the main church until relatively recently, when it was lost and replaced by a porcelain replica. The other, larger in size, and rougher-hewn, now resides in the nearby chapel. Another version, supported by church historians, is that a young Indian girl saw flames coming from a guaje tree near the present day site of San Pedro Tesistán, on the southern side of the lake. Branches of the tree were later carved into these two statues and one other which is now in private hands.

For many years, the statue in the main church was kept in the church baptistry

El Mesón de los Naranjitos

The route of Highway 15 from Mexico City gave Jocotepec the distinction of being the fifth and last overnight stopping place on the stage-coach route to Guadalajara. As a result, for much of its 150-year history, the hotel was known as La Quinta. The through-traffic guaranteed a regular income not only to the hotel but also to the town's "ladies of the night" and others.

To ensure that benefits from this passing trade were maximised, the hotel had strict rules including *"No se permite que entre pastura"* ("Guests are not allowed to bring hay"), meaning that only the hotel could furnish the traveller's exhausted horses with the hay necessary for their feed.

During the Mexican Revolution in 1910, some of the first fighting in Jalisco was at El Mesón de los Naranjitos, but it was not over politics but over a love affair. A secret passageway is rumoured to have existed at the time, used perhaps by bandits listening for the latest news of the gold-laden pack trains which passed along the main road.... Later, in 1959, the Mexican President-elect, Adolfo López Mateos, visited the hotel and the final stretch of the Chapala-Jocotepec road was paved on the very morning of his visit.

The hotel was a typical adobe building with a tiled roof, shuttered windows and wrought-iron work. Inside, the first patio had a huge tree growing in the middle with a stand of bamboo to one side. The furniture was local *equipales* and what was visible of the floor, rustic tiles. The guestrooms had fireplaces, low doorways (the kind you bang your head on) and the sheets on the beds weren't long enough to be properly tucked in.

Naturally, as with any old building, there's plenty of talk of ghosts. And whether you believe in them or not, wouldn't it be interesting to know more about those three men in black sarapes and tall hats who, one night in May, walked through a wall? And what about those mysterious noises associated with Room 3?

The building, drastically modified in the 1980's, stands on the corner of Miguel Arana and Matamoros streets.

• • •

near the main doors. It was rehung above the main altar after gaining fame as being "miraculous", credited with the speedy ending of cholera outbreaks in 1833 and 1850 and a Spanish influenza epidemic in 1918, as well as with numerous personal miracles. This statue was paraded ceremoniously up the mountain side every Easter and became known as "El Señor del Monte" (The Lord of the Mountain).

In the smaller, simpler chapel is the statue which historians claim was the first to be carved from the guaje tree: "El Señor del Guaje". Years ago, when the local priest tried to prize it off the wall, intending to replace it with a more modern figure, he was unable to do so, hence its nickname, "The Immovable One". The chapel is probably older than the main church and may well be seventeenth century.

Each of the two central churches has given rise to a town fiesta. The larger fiesta, in honour of "El Señor del Monte", begins in early January and lasts two weeks. There are daily masses, dances, cockfights, bullfights, parades with floats, and fireworks, and the town centre is transformed into a gigantic street market-cum-fairground with children's rides, a Ferris wheel, stalls selling food, novelties, and household items. The last evening of the fiesta, always a Sunday, becomes an enormous, joyous street-party for the entire town. Like most village fiestas, each day's entertainment is financed by a different group of local people: one day may be the responsibility of the shopkeepers, another of the stonemasons and bricklayers, another of the textile workers, and so on. The final evening is usually reserved for the returning migrants from the U.S., since they have more money than most of the resident townspeople. The last night's fireworks tower or *castillo* has to be seen to be believed – just don't stand too close.

Later in the year comes the fiesta for "El Señor del Guaje" with similar events, fun and noise, albeit on a marginally smaller scale.

A short walk from the plaza is a building which has one of the most interesting histories of any lakeside building. Years before the advent of tourism in Chapala, the La Quinta hotel was serving as the last overnight stop for travellers going from Mexico City to Guadalajara.

One of its former owners, Allen W. Lloyd, was instrumental in reviving Jocotepec's traditional *sarape* (riding blanket) industry. Many guide books refer to the "famous white sarapes" of the town although, actually, they were never entirely white, but had black or grey designs or coloured flower motifs on them. Excellent woven blankets, sarapes, and wall-hangings are still produced in the town. Several of the shops along Hidalgo street sell them and it is also possible to visit the houses of the artisans, who make them on handlooms, to commission a design of your own choosing for that special gift.

Still on an artistic note, several years ago, the internationally famous Austrian artist, Georg Rauch, built his home a short distance east of the town, overlooking both town and lake. He and his wife Phyllis, also an exhibiting artist, enjoy meeting serious art collectors and showing them round their studios. Ask for

The Hat Shop

directions, or look for the signs.

And, before leaving Jocotepec, it is worth considering a visit to the Special Education Centre and/or the Development Centre. It's an extraordinary claim-to-fame for a small Mexican town, but both of these social welfare projects have received the highest praise internationally. The Special Education Centre, on Privada Gonzalez Ortega and open mornings during term time, began life as the Lakeside School for the Deaf. Pioneering the education of hearing-impaired youngsters in rural areas, it grew so quickly under the direction of deaf educator Gwen Chan that fundraising couldn't keep pace with demand. Happily, the state government offered to assume financial responsibility. Chan is now setting up an audiological support system for students throughout the country. Sylvia Flores, director of the Development Centre, at 173 Vicente Guerrero East, has been invited on several occasions to address U.N. conferences on rural development and family planning. Flores' project, which has established family health clinics in several lakeside communities, has already made a real difference to hundreds of families in the region. Visiting any of these projects offers a unique glimpse into local life.

From Jocotepec, a short drive northwards across the flat floor of the Zapotitán valley, once a tributary arm of Lake Chapala, brings you to the small villages of Zapotitán and Huejotitán, both former haciendas. The Zapotitan ex-hacienda, which dates from the mid-nineteenth century, has an unusual mural map. A children's home now occupies Huejotitan's old Great House. Any of the staff will happily show visitors around this historic and well-maintained property.

• • •

The north shore from Tuxcueca

5. The South Side of the Lake
Scenic and Undeveloped

What a shame that more people do not drive along the southern shoreline. This side of the lake, the road keeps close to the water opening up vistas far superior to anything from the northern shore.

This is the undeveloped, some would say unspoiled side, with small fishing villages where the people live much as they did at the time of the Revolution. The smell of wood-smoke fires drifts through open car windows, sheep and cows graze contentedly by the roadside and, depending on the season, the wildflowers bloom in profusion.

The route is also a recommendable alternative for trips into any part of the neighbouring state of Michoacán since it avoids the crowded Guadalajara-La Barca-Zamora highway. This older lakeshore route, Highway 15, also goes to Zamora but the driving and scenery are far more relaxing.

Almost all the small villages along this road keep quietly to one side; they refuse to give up their secrets to travellers in a hurry. From Jocotepec, the first is San Pedro Tesistán, where fine *equipal* furniture is made. Then come San Cristóbal Zapotitlán, San Luis Soyatlán (here the road makes a rare exception, going alongside the plaza and market), San Nicolás, Tepeguaje... And then comes Tuxcueca with its ancient church sitting atop a rocky knoll that was once an island in the lake. All these village names have intriguing etymologies, but perhaps none more so than Tuxcueca, which is derived from "the hubbub of rabbits" or "where they make petticoats of rabbit-hair".

Here is the junction for the road to Mazamitla (chapter 14). A short distance beyond the junction is Puruagua, birthplace of General Ramón Corona, a distinguished soldier and politician of the nineteenth century. A small bronze bust at the side of the highway ensures that he is not forgotten. Ramón Corona, while

The Water Hyacinth or "*Lirio*"

The beautiful violet and yellow flowers of the water hyacinth (*Eichhornia crassipes*) add an attractive splash of colour in the Lake Chapala landscape during the rainy season but the "lirio" as the locals call it, is often considered a problem.

The water hyacinth, a native of Brazil, was introduced to adorn the fish ponds of haciendas at the eastern end of Lake Chapala at the end of the nineteenth century. It now prospers on the steady supply of fertilizers and soil washed into the lake. Its air-filled leaves and stems enable it to float around the lake from one side to the other, depending on the wind.

In only a single growing season, 25 plants can multiply to become two million separate plants, covering up to 10,000 square metres of water surface. In Lake Chapala, up to 20% of the water surface may be covered in some years, less than 2% in others

The water hyacinth blocks canals, hinders navigation and decreases the amount of dissolved oxygen in the water, endangering fish stocks. Dense mats of hyacinth create ideal microhabitats for undesirable organisms such as mosquito larvae.

There is only one unexpected benefit of this otherwise noxious weed: it filters from the lake harmful heavy metals such as mercury and lead, brought in by the river Lerma; the Lerma collects them from the residual wastes of industries operating along its banks.

How can it be controlled? Cutting it only serves to help it propagate, and can rarely keep pace with the increased growth. Chemicals affect water quality and have their own deleterious effects on fish stocks. The introduction of manatees or "sea-cows" to control the hyacinth was successful in Guyana but in Chapala, they were quickly fished to extinction. In Lake Chapala, there seems to be a natural cycle to the cover of water hyacinth which we are powerless to alter to any significant degree with currently available methods.

• • •

Governor of Jalisco, was assassinated by the aptly named Primitivo Ron in 1889, but not before gaining glory for himself and his followers by defeating Manuel Lozada, the "Tiger of Alica", in the Battle of La Mojonera at a site just outside Guadalajara. For many years, the 28th of January was an official state holiday in celebration of this victory.

Near Tizapán el Alto, the scenery changes. The Passion River has brought tonnes of mud into the lake and its fertile delta has been converted into rich farmland, used for growing vegetables such as onions, green beans and cabbages. Along the edge of the lake are swampy areas, sometimes cultivable if lake levels are low, at other times reclaimed by the lake for its reeds, which serve as refuges for thousands of aquatic birds including flocks of white pelicans.

The town of Tizapán is by far the largest on the southern shore and was chosen as the site of one of Jalisco's model *ejidos*. The ejidos were created after the Mexican Revolution. The idea was to split up the huge landholdings of the former haciendas into smaller family-sized plots. Unfortunately, in many cases the land given to the villagers was marginal at best and the size of their holdings was insufficient to do more than eke out the barest of existences. The model ejido here is marked by an iron archway. As the road climbs past it, the small size and rough nature of the small holdings becomes apparent. Here is a village without a centre, *campesinos* without adequate land.

The next part of the drive is beautiful, my favourite part of the entire lakeshore. The vast lake is revealed in all its glory. The hills sharply visible in the distance mark the northern shore, and Scorpion and Mezcala islands stand guard over the local fishermen in their small boats.

There is a curiosity here, too, for the observant. The road goes between two stone towers, the symbol adopted by the state of Michoacán, many years ago, to mark its boundaries. But, even if Michoacán is convinced its boundary line runs this far west, Jalisco, supported by the Federal Roads Department, certainly isn't. Two kilometres further east are signs clearly marking their idea of where the boundary line goes. Who knows what the residents in the disputed area between these boundaries do for state taxes? Do they pay double, or none at all? To further compound the curiosity, many official maps show a third, completely different, position for the Michoacán-Jalisco boundary at this point.

Safely inside Michoacán by any definition, the village of Petatán has the most photogenic setting of all the lakeside villages. Its houses crowd around a prominent church; all are on an impossibly small rocky outcrop, once an island. A narrow causeway links the village to the main road.

Petatán is the centre of Lake Chapala's *charal* fishing industry. The *charal,* a small, sardine-like cousin of the whitefish, is either deep-fried or sun-dried and eaten whole as an appetizer, with hot sauce and slices of fresh lime. During winter, the bay to the east of the village becomes home-from-home for several hundred migrant white pelicans, who obviously agree with the fishermen about the best place to catch their dinner.

The domed church of Cojumatlán is also a local landmark, and worth a glance inside. Its marble floor and pillars are a suitable backdrop for large and colourful religious paintings. The village of Cojumatlán is a strange mixture of the old and the new. Opposite the crumbling municipal building with its ceremonial bell, is an office advertising public fax service.

As the road climbs steeply from Cojumatlán, a startling view unfolds of an arm of the lake, which once harboured pirates, and unexpectedly vast expanses of flat fields. All this flat area was once under the lake. This is but one small part of the area which was deliberately drained for agriculture less than a hundred years ago. The 1900 shoreline of the lake went as far east as Ixtlán de los Hervores and as far south as Jiquilpan. The drainage scheme was justified by the extraordinary claim that reducing the lake's area would reduce its losses through evaporation, thus increasing its volume of water!

Just outside Sahuayo, a lively commercial centre, is State Highway 5 to Briseñas and La Barca (chapter 7) for those who want to circumnavigate the lake. Ten minutes beyond Sahuayo is the fascinating town of Jiquilpan.

● ● ●

6. Jiquilpan
More than its Fair Share of Mexican Heritage

For a small Mexican town of somewhat nondescript architecture, Jiquilpan de Juárez, in Michoacán, has considerable claim to fame. Birthplace of two Mexican Presidents, who played pivotal roles in national affairs, and several distinguished artists, Jiquilpan's unprepossessing exterior appearance offers no hint of the important works of art – including sculptures and a singular mural – which are to be discovered in the town.

The first former Mexican President associated with the town is Anastacio Bustamante, who had the distinction of being President twice. In between times, Mexico was forced to cede a large part of its territory, including Texas, to the United States. Bustamante, considered one of the more honest nineteenth century politicians, seized power for the first time in 1830, overthrowing Vicente Guerrero. He was in turn overthrown by Santa Anna in 1832, and fled to England. On resuming office in 1837, after the rather unsavory incidents which robbed Mexico of Texas, Bustamante immediately faced the "Pastry War" crisis. Eventful times!

Lázaro Cárdenas was born in the town on the 21st May, 1895. As a boy, he worked in a printery, and later a rent office, in his native town; not yet twenty years old, he played a significant role in the Mexican Revolution, and subsequently became Governor of Michoacán. As national President (1934-40), he presided over a massive agrarian reform programme and, in 1938, the nationalisation of the railways and the oil industry. He was the last President to be held in sufficient esteem to occupy important ministerial posts including Defense Secretary after his term as President ended.

On Jiquilpan's main street, appropriately named Avenida Lázaro Cárdenas, are the library and the town museum. During Lázaro Cárdenas' presidency, a nineteenth century church in Jiquilpan was converted to a library and embellished with two impressive works of art. The new door of the library, in which are sculpted the heads of 22 of the most outstanding figures of the early twentieth century, was designed by Guillermo Ruiz. It is a beautiful tribute to the greatest thinkers and scientists of the time (Edison, Marti, etc.). Ruiz is perhaps better known for his monumental (40 metres high) statue of Morelos on the island of Janitzio in Lake Pátzcuaro.

An even more prominent figure in the history of Mexican art, José Clemente Orozco, was responsible for the murals decorating the interior of the library. Orozco was one of the famous "Big Three" of Mexican Muralism, the others being Diego Rivera and David Alfaro Siqueiros. Orozco painted, literally single-handedly (having lost his left hand in a childhood accident) a series of sketchy black-and-white murals depicting political parties and revolutionary Mexico on either side of the former nave and an unusual and striking full-colour mural known as "A Mexican Allegory" on the end wall. Painted in 1940, it is one of his last com-pleted works. Whatever meaning he intended, and it should be pointed out that Orozco himself rarely volunteered explanations of his work, the mural is full of symbols which beg a coherent interpretation. Justino Fernández, professor and art critic, offered the following interpretation: The jaguar, centrally placed in the mural, represents the Mexican people. It is walking on *nopales* (prickly pears), suggesting suffering and an inability to find an alternative path. Seated on the jaguar is La Patria

The Pastry War

The Pastry War began when Mexico refused to pay compensation for damages to a pastry shop, owned by a Frenchman in Mexico City. The shop had allegedly been looted during riots in 1828.

Ten years later, the French government used this pretext, and other losses which had occured at the same time to other French property, to demand 600,000 dollars in damages from the Mexican government of Bustamante. The French also sought a preferential trading agreement with Mexico.

Bustamante considered the claim for looted pastries to be preposterous and refused either to pay, or to consider the trade agreement. Outraged, the French brought up a fleet from the Caribbean island of Martinique and blockaded Veracruz.

Seven months later, the French added a further 200,000 dollars to their demand to cover the costs of the blockade. Bustamante finally gave in and paid in full, whereupon the French fleet sailed off.

• • •

symbolising hope. Above are an eagle and a serpent which were, of course, central to Aztec cosmology. On the right are three kings – the three princes of the local Purépecha tribe or the three principal upheavals in modern Mexican history, Independence, Reform and Revolution? Why not see it for yourself and decide what you think? The library is closed at lunchtime and on Sundays.

Jiquilpan museum is a modern building and includes a collection of archaeological pieces unearthed from a nearby shaft-tomb. Shaft-tombs, hollowed out deep underground and reached typically by a vertical shaft, are thought to have been reserved for the nobility (page 101). They predate the Spanish conquest by some two thousand years and the offerings left in them have provided valuable insights into life in pre-Columbian times. The Loma de Otero tomb contained a unique stone stool among many other beautiful finds.

In addition to the archaeological pieces, the museum is now the home of the "Centre for Studies of the Mexican Revolution". Even non-Spanish speakers can gain insights into the turbulent and complex times that comprise the Mexican Revolution by looking at the extensive photographic exhibition on the museum's first floor. The exhibition details the life and works not only of Lázaro Cárdenas but also of other key figures in twentieth century Mexican politics including General Francisco Múgica, who was in the group which proposed for inclusion in the Constitution of 1917, (still current today), Article 27 which encompassed agrarian reform and land redistribution, and Article 123 which dealt with the rights of workers, including an eight-hour day and guaranteed minimum wages. The museum in Jiquilpan is a fitting tribute to these much revered politicians.

Other natives of Jiquilpan have also made their mark in national affairs. The artist Feliciano Bejar, still active today, is revered for his inspiring sculptures, painting and weaving. Many of his pieces imaginatively combine glass with metals and plastics and his most famous series of works, called "magiscopes" succeed in making the viewer aware of the unlimited power of the human eye to see and interpret abstract sculptures.

Also to be discovered in Jiquilpan are a statue of Christ on the Cross, said to date from the times of Emperor Charles V (now in San Francisco church), and a fountain sculpted by Francisco Eduardo Tresguerras, Mexico's most famous nineteenth century sculptor and architect. This fountain was originally on the El Cabezón hacienda in Jalisco (page 59), but was then lost – until it mysteriously reappeared, years later, in Jiquilpan.

The ancient hieroglyph for Jiquilpan, from pre-Columbian times, is a horizontal line of earth with two indigo plants above it, linking the town to the colour blue. One of the town's most famous sons, Roberto Villaseñor Espinoza, also linked his birthplace to the colour blue. Tragically, "El Ticolín", as he was nicknamed, lost his life in the September 1985 Mexico City earthquakes. As poet and song-writer, however, he had already made a lasting contribution to Jiquilpan's imagery by

Entrance to Guaracha

christening it, "the city of jacarandas", a term still used today. And anyone who drives through the town during jacaranda-season (February-March) will certainly agree that the tall trees with their lavender-blue blossoms bordering the main avenues are a magnificent sight.

A Huge Hacienda

A few kilometres east of Jiquilpan, along Highway 15, is the village of Emiliano Zapata, formerly Guaracha, once one of the biggest haciendas in Western Mexico. It was first established at the end of the sixteenth century and eventually came to control an area of 920 square kilometres, equivalent to about half the size of Lake Chapala. Black slaves were imported to work the fields; their owners became renowned for their cruelty. The hacienda was sufficiently powerful both to persuade the railway company to give them their own station in 1901 and to control the supply of water after this part of Lake Chapala had been deliberately drained for agriculture in 1905.

Whatever the agricultural efficiency of haciendas in the nineteenth century, there is no doubt that they kept their workforces enslaved by debt, rather than by bondage. The main means of guaranteeing this dependence and indebtedness was the *tienda de raya* (the hacienda store). Guaracha was finally broken up in 1936, a long time after the Revolution.

Today, visitors entering the village from the west first see the ruins of the former sugar mill with its tall chimney stack. This was the factory part of the operation.

Round a curve in the road and, atop a small hill, stands a lovely old building with interior patios and graceful arches. From here a superb view extends over a fertile valley which, only a little over a hundred years ago, was a shallow arm of Lake Chapala. The building, now used as a school, was the Great House, or hacienda owner's residence. To its left is the small private chapel which family members would have used. To its right, across a tiny plaza, are the single-storey dwellings which were their workers' homes.

The gardens of the Great House originally occupied the area on the other side of the present highway. One of the signs throughout Western Mexico of former hacienda gardens is the presence of exotic (i.e. imported) plants and trees. Sure enough, here at Guaracha, the old gardens are clearly delimited by tall palm trees which once presided over a regal layout of formal lawns and flower beds.

Mud Volcanoes

Going a long way further back in time, but only a few kilometres further east along the highway, are the extraordinary Los Negritos (the Little Black Ones), a legacy left by the ancient volcanic nature of all this area.

Los Negritos are small mud volcanoes (up to a metre or two across) which burble and gurgle, hiss and splutter, and occasionally erupt, throwing hot mud into the air and emitting sulphurous fumes. They are great fun to watch, but take care! Don't get too close or you may be splattered with the hot mud or, worse yet, you may step in the innocuous-looking but highly unstable surrounding mud patches which can rarely hold a person's weight.

The all-weather dirt road to Los Negritos begins at Villamar, twelve kilometres east of Jiquilpan. Ask for directions as you drive through the village. The mud volcanoes are about two kilometres to the north, near an attractive lake and an isolated clump of conifers. This is excellent bird-watching country – look particularly for the spectacular vermilion flycatcher.

• • •

7. The Eastern End of the Lake
An Area Worth Exploring

The Stones and Stories of La Barca

The town of La Barca has one of the most fascinating histories of any town in the state of Jalisco, and this history is still very visible in its architecture and layout. Its name, "The Boat", takes us back to the sixteenth century when the Spanish conquistadors came westwards from central Mexico into this region of the country. The major obstacle to increased trade and communication between the capital of New Spain, Mexico City, and the capital of New Galicia, Guadalajara, was the River Lerma, the only major river entering Lake Chapala.

People crossed the Lerma using a boat, or more precisely, a canoe, big enough to hold 14 people, and their goods and animals. A small settlement, La Barca, quickly grew up around the landing stage, with dwellings offering food, water and overnight accommodation.

La Barca was formally designated a town in 1553. It was laid out following the usual Spanish colonial town-planning rules such as streets at right angles, north-south and east-west, and a central square big enough for displays of horsemanship.

In 1810, at the start of the Mexican War of Independence, Father Miguel Hidalgo rode through the town with his followers on his way to Guadalajara. In a passionate speech in La Barca, the eloquent priest demanded an end to slavery, a demand he made law only a few days later. In 1824, shortly after Mexico was granted independence, La Barca was elevated to city status.

A small but beautiful mid-seventeenth century chapel, San Nicolás de Tolentino, on Morelos street, dates from these early days. It is a remodelled Augustinian building with a neoclassic altar. Just around the corner, on the main square, stands the town hall. Its seventeenth century lower storey is 300 years older than its new upper storey. Its *portales* (arcades) were considered some of the finest in the country. Unfortunately, their profile has been drastically changed by this recent addition, horrible, tasteless, and out of character.

Just off the northwest corner of the plaza is the imposing Santa Monica Church which was built at the end of the eighteenth century. Its baroque façade and spacious single nave are typical of the period. Strangely enough, the Virgin above the altar is not the statue of Santa Monica, but the brown-skinned Virgin of Tepeyac.

A corner property across from the church is occupied by La Moreña, a charming period town-house with interior patios and high ceilings, built in the

"El Burro de Oro – The Golden Ass"

José Francisco Velarde, born in 1820, owned the haciendas of Buenavista, Cumuato and San José, the town-house of La Moreña in La Barca, and a city residence in Guadalajara, on the main plaza. The area he owned was equivalent to a small state in its own right.

Velarde's misguided political ambitions and ostentatious love of wealth led one outspoken chronicler to call him "as rich as he was ignorant"..."a golden ass"! This epithet sums him up better than most. Velarde's house in La Barca boasted a wealth of imported items – furniture and perfumes among them – and he habitually wore gold buttons and carried a gold walking stick. He maintained a harem of assorted locals, mixed-race women and black former slaves.

In the 1860's, Velarde paid US $50,000 for permission to form his own private army in support of the French Intervention in Mexico and Emperor Maximilian.

Maximilian and his wife, Carlotta, arrived in Mexico in 1864 and are supposed to have asked immediately, "And who is the rancher prince?", referring to none other than donkey-brain Velarde. It is possible that the two men actually met, and it is likely that Velarde's sumptuous decoration of La Moreña with European-style murals, was part of his preparations for receiving Maximilian in his country-seat one day.

Unfortunately for both men, Maximilian lasted only until 1867, when he was captured and executed in Querétaro. Velarde, in turn, was captured in Zamora, and despite offering over one million dollars for a pardon, was shot on June 14th, 1867. Ironically, he died even before Maximilian's own execution was carried out.

His extensive land-holdings, instead of passing to his wife, Nicolasa, and his three children, were confiscated by the government.

• • •

1850's. On the walls enclosing the patios, a series of unique nineteenth century murals have caused La Moreña to be designated a museum. Nowhere else in the country can you find such well preserved (and well restored) examples of the decoration of the fashionable private dwellings favoured by the rich land owners, or *hacendados* of the time.

The mansion was built and owned by José Francisco Velarde, an exceedingly colourful character. Velarde may have commissioned the paintings in preparation for a visit by Maximilian, the Hapsburg Emperor who had been given the Mexican crown in 1864 by Napoleon III of France. The artistic authorship of these wonderful murals is still the subject of debate, despite the plaque at the museum's entrance attributing them to Gerardo Suárez. Suárez, a well-known Jaliscan artist of the time, died tragically young. His teacher, Jacobo Gálvez, the architect of the Degollado Theatre in Guadalajara, is the other likely candidate for having painted the murals, though some art scholars argue that another member of his family, Francisco Gálvez, may also have worked on them.

Whatever their provenance, they are magnificent works, painted, according to twentieth century restorers, in a mixture of milk, vegetable dyes and blood! Most of the scenes derive from lithographs published in *Mexico and its Surroundings,* printed in 1855-56. The murals include Mexico City scenes such as the Santo Domingo plaza, and Xochimilco and its canals, the Party, Children (notice the child holding a rat by its tail) and the very Jaliscan *jarabe tapatío* dance.

The mansion fell into disuse and became a billiard hall and a *cantina* (bar) before being restored and opened as a museum. Besides the murals, the museum houses a collection of local artifacts and has rooms reserved for temporary exhibitions.

A few yards from the centre of La Barca, past the town's market, is a small park overlooking the river Lerma. Fierro, a local poet, was probably standing here when he penned the following lines:

"City of happy bearing and sumptuous form
In perpetual romance with the river
Where clear is the light, golden the dew,
And blue the sky which blankets the valley."

And fifty years ago, before indiscriminate use of its water by Mexico City, and for industry and agriculture along its course, this river must have been a very pretty sight, though perhaps a rather daunting one to early travellers. Today, the river is only a trickle of its former self and is regularly covered with the pretty purple flowers of the water hyacinth which choke its course. Periodic clearance campaigns are carried out in an effort to maintain the flow of water along the river into Lake Chapala, so essential to the lake's well-being.

On the other side of the river lies Briseñas, the somewhat scruffy town where the round-the-lake road joins the main Morelia-Guadalajara highway. Twenty-five kilometres beyond Briseñas is the geyser of Ixtlán de los Hervores. At Ixtlán

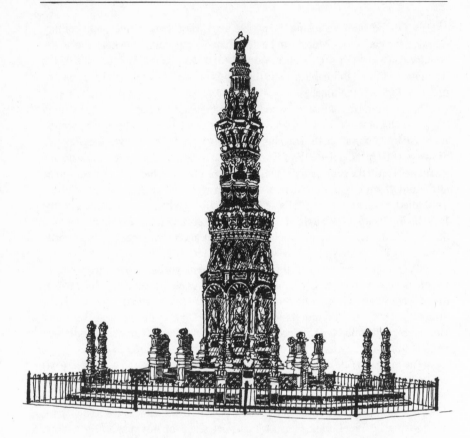

Monument to Pope Pius IX

the water temperature is 95°C, more than sufficient to cook breakfast eggs. Ixtlán mud-packs on sale at the entrance to the small park are reputed to have great therapeutic powers. Legend has it that the Tarascan princess, Atzimba, as part of her initiation ceremony, had to take two baths, one in the cold waters of Lake Camécuaro (page 149) and the other, which presumably was more of a shower than a bath, in the geyser of Ixtlán. This initiation ceremony is not recommended for anyone other than real princesses.

Jamay – Monument to a Pope

Rarely does a single monument make a town, but Jamay is clearly the exception that proves the rule. From the town plaza rises one of the largest and most extraordinary monuments in the entire state of Jalisco.

Thirty-five metres high, built between 1875 and 1879, of *cantera* (sandstone) and erected by a local priest, José María Zárate, it tells the story of the then Pope,

Pius IX. The lower part details his biography, including his birth on 13th May 1792, his appointment as Archbishop of Spoletto in 1827 and his imprisonment by King Victor Manuel in 1870; the upper part describes his works as Pope including his defense of the Immaculate Conception and his defining of the dogma, "The Pope is infallible". Few towns outside Italy and the Vatican can possibly boast papal monuments on this scale; perhaps none so much resembles the decoration on a wedding-cake. Sadly, the priest responsible for this monument paid for it by selling the superb baroque high altar of his eighteenth century parish church; its whereabouts today are unknown. On the eastern side of the plaza is a stone sundial donated to the town by Augustine fathers in 1766.

There are several good places to eat between Jamay and Ocotlán. Just opposite Luminarias restaurant, a narrow track north of the highway leads to a quarry where you can admire basaltic prisms and columns, reminiscent of Giant's Causeway in Ireland or Devil's Postpile in the U.S.

Ocotlán – Site of a Miracle

Ocotlán, one of the largest lakeside towns, is located where the only river which drains the lake, the Santiago, flows off to the north towards Juanacatlán falls and Guadalajara. Its name simply means "the Indian village near the pine tree". Legend has it that next to the pine tree was a hut with a stone idol, much adored by the natives. On the town square, the older of the two churches, the Chapel of the Conception, is a sixteenth century Franciscan chapel, rebuilt by the Augustines in the seventeenth century; its exterior has been restored to its former glory. It was one of the few buildings to survive the disastrous earthquake which struck the town on the 2nd of October, 1847.

The next day, at the open-air mass celebrated in the plaza for the survivors, a resplendent cloud suddenly appeared in an otherwise blue sky, producing a vision, seen by thousands, of Christ on the Cross. The site of the mass is now marked by an obelisk. David Cardona and Francisco Sánchez del Castillo later painted a series of fine large works depicting the earthquake, the vision and the hearings held afterwards to establish its authenticity. The paintings can be admired today in Ocotlán's spacious new nineteenth century church dedicated to "Our Lord of Mercy".

Two blocks south of the plaza is a small museum, well worth a brief visit. It has a good collection of local archaeological pieces and a series of photographs showing the details of rock-carvings, laboriously chipped out by local Indians at about the time of the Spanish conquest; the original petroglyphs are mostly on virtually inaccessible mountain sides. The museum also has a large-scale replica of a typical Lake Chapala sail-canoe. In the nineteenth century, such sail-canoes were the principal means of transportation used on the lake.

There is an interesting historical mural in the town hall, midway between the museum and the plaza, and the fishermen's church, "El Refugio", merits more than a passing glance.

Poncitlán – A Sixteenth Century Icon

Between Ocotlán and Guadalajara is the town of Poncitlán, which was a very important settlement in pre-Columbian times. On its plaza stands the convent of Saint Peter and Saint Paul, founded as early as 1533. Inside, above the altar, is an ancient, sixteenth century statue of the Virgin Mary, "Our Lady of the Rosary", one of four identical statues brought from the Old World to the New in 1548, on the direct orders of King Charles V of Spain. The other three statues were all sent to Guadalajara but only two of them – those in the Cathedral and in the church of Santa Monica – have survived to the present day. The third was destroyed in 1936 when an arsonist set fire to the magnificent altarpiece of the San Francisco Church.

Poncitlán celebrates its religious fiesta, in honour, naturally, of Our Lady of the Rosary, for nine days ending on the third Sunday in November. The town is also renowned for its miniature tea-sets.

• • •

Juanacatlán Falls

"The Niagara of Mexico" is a natural waterfall on the River Santiago as it winds its way northwards from Lake Chapala to the Oblatos Canyon, the deep ravine which skirts around the northern edge of the city of Guadalajara. Between the small villages of El Salto (The Waterfall) and Juanacatlán, 17 kilometres east of the Guadalajara-Chapala highway, is the second biggest waterfall in North America, the biggest being Niagara. A bridge with 24 arches spans the falls and links the two villages.

The falls became part of Mexican postal history in 1899 when they became the first landscape ever depicted on a Mexican postage stamp – previously only people or emblems had been used. Mexican philatelic experts consider this set, designed and printed in England, which also included views of Popocatepetl and Mexico City cathedral, one of the veritable gems of Mexican postal issues. A magnifying glass is needed to appreciate the astonishing detail on these small stamps.

The Juanacatlán falls are shown as a waterfall of immense beauty, a description echoed by contemporary tourist guides which speak of a "magnificent spectacle" and the "majestic falls".

Despite their fame, the 35 metre high falls were reduced in the 1980's to a dribble of dirty, evil-smelling effluent. At the turn of the century the falls provided hydro-electric power for Guadalajara and turned the wheels of a cotton and woollen mill, whose empty shell stands to one side.

Hopefully one day these historic falls will be restored to their rightful place as one of Mexico's greatest tourist attractions.

• • •

8. Cajititlán and its Fiesta

E very January one of the most popular and spectacular village fiestas in Western Mexico takes place in the small village of Cajititlán, near Guadalajara's International Airport. The fiesta begins on December 31st and reaches its climax in a blaze of colour and fireworks on January 6th. Tens of thousands of people (but few non-Mexicans) attend this memorable celebration which is held in honour of the village's patron saints, the Three Kings (or Three Wise Men).

In the old days, this fiesta used to last three months, but nowadays, a week is considered sufficient. The Cajititlán fiesta is still a monumental affair. Visitors have to park at the entrance to the village, some five or six blocks from the plaza. Some of the dozens of *puestos* (stalls) lining the village streets sell food, beverages, and trinkets. Others are devoted to favourite pastimes such as throwing darts at balloons, shooting galleries, and other such entertainments.

The central plaza is jammed with onlookers trying to catch a glimpse of the folkloric dancing or, near 5:00 pm, hoping to be in a good position to witness the daily procession bearing the Three Kings around the village and back to their church. The participants in both the dancing and the procession wear the most amazing costumes. The more intricate are astonishingly colourful and must have taken the entire year since the last fiesta to make. In the evening, fireworks, including fabulous *castillos* (towers), light up the night sky with brilliant patterns, revealing the most astounding skill of the *cohetero,* or fireworks maker. Invariably some of the hoped-for effects fizzle out before they are supposed to and some parts of the structure fly off into the crowd, scattering people in all directions, leaving incandescent trails of sparks and smoke.

The Cajititlán fiesta is an absolute riot of sights, sounds, and smells. Food, some of it recognizable, some not, is sizzling on charcoal burners. It may smell delicious, but taste it at your own risk since some is prepared in less than hygienic conditions. Real fiesta *aficionados* swear that you never get sick as long as you chase any food with a sufficient quantity of strong tequila, as the locals do. Even a short time spent witnessing a fiesta will convince you that whatever else Mexicans may do, they certainly know how to enjoy themselves when given the opportunity and excuse.

The church is the main centre of activity with several masses held each day and a long line of penitents queuing to touch or kiss one of the Three Kings in the belief that they will then have improved luck or health in the coming year. Many of those who come to Cajititlán for the fiesta are from far-away villages. Some literally crawl the last yards toward the altar on their knees in penance.

The jostling crowds of the fiesta make it impossible to appreciate the details of the church, which is a superb example of seventeenth century religious architecture. Unlike many Mexican churches which look impressive from the outside but have little of interest within, this church has an interior even more worthy of

Three Kings Day – January 6th

In the Christian calendar, the sixth of January (Epiphany) is the day when the magi arrived in Bethlehem with their gifts for the infant Jesus. The original Mexican gift-giving tradition at Christmas time was to exchange presents on Three Kings Day, and not, as elsewhere, on Christmas Day. This century the tradition has broken down in the face of the enormous consumer-oriented publicity from north of the border, which stresses Christmas (rather than Epiphany) gifts. Some greedy Mexican middle class children now expect to receive gifts on both days, claiming that parents and grandparents should not only preserve the old customs but also embrace the new version.

Even if gifts are no longer exchanged, January 6th is still very much a family day in Mexico. In the early afternoon, or at supper time, it is traditional to share a *rosca* or two. Roscas are ring-shaped loaves of sweet bread, sold and eaten on special occasions. The roscas eaten on Three Kings Day contain a small plastic (formerly ceramic) *muñeco* (doll). Whoever happens to choose or be given the piece of rosca containing it has to throw a party for everyone present, on February 2nd, *Día de La Candelaria*, Candlemas day. In some parts of Mexico this is less fun for the party giver than you might think, since his guests will expect to be served home-made *mole*, a sauce which contains dozens of ingredients including nuts, chocolate and numerous spices, and which takes many hours of preparation.

• • •

close examination than its imposing exterior. The statues of the Three Kings, made of mesquite wood, were carved by local craftsmen over four hundred years ago in 1587. The southern chapel has a magnificent, gilded *retablo* (altarpiece) behind its plateresque altar with some fine examples of colonial religious paintings. All in all, a truly magnificent example of ecclesiastical art and architecture.

Across the square is an even older architectural gem, dating from 1561: a small baroque chapel, dedicated to the Virgin of Guadalupe, which the Franciscans constructed on the northern shore of Cajititlán lake.

The locals all claim that their eight kilometre (five mile) long lake is much nicer, cleaner and deeper than Lake Chapala, and they're probably right. They are also very proud of their recently renovated plaza which is a lovely illustration of how progress can respect the existing character of a place, even while rendering it more accessible and more functional. Standing in the plaza today (but not on January 6th), it's easy to travel several hundred years back in time, and imagine life in Cajititlán as it was when Spain still ruled Texas, California, Mexico, and a good chunk of the rest of Central and South America besides....

Cajititlán is nine kilometres west of Highway 23, past the Guadalajara autodrome. This road, which continues on to San Miguel Cuyutlán, at the western end of the lake, is a very pretty drive, especially during the rainy season. All the route is paved, except for a very short section near San Miguel. From San Miguel, you can either continue by paved road westwards to Tlajomulco de Zúñiga and Highway 54, or drive around the southern shore of the lake, on a cobblestone road, to the villages of San Lucas and San Juan Evangelista.

These two villages have highly ornate Franciscan churches decorated in the flowery, exuberant, *primitivismo* style known as Jaliscan Popular Baroque, the happy result of indigenous stonemasons being given free rein by their ecclesiastical employers. Only a few churches in Western Mexico display this ornate architectural style, and most are located in the area between Lake Chapala and Guadalajara.

From San Juan Evangelista, the cobblestone road continues to Santa Rosa on Highway 23.

An excursion to Lake Cajititlán and its villages is a pleasant way to pass a morning or afternoon, whether or not it is fiesta time. Why not see for yourself villages that suggest another side of Mexico to the one normally seen by tourists? Standing in Cajititlán's large open plaza gives you an opportunity to appreciate the serenity and grandeur of a seventeenth century colonial town centre, or, if you visit in January, a lively experience of *"Mexicanismo"*.

• • •

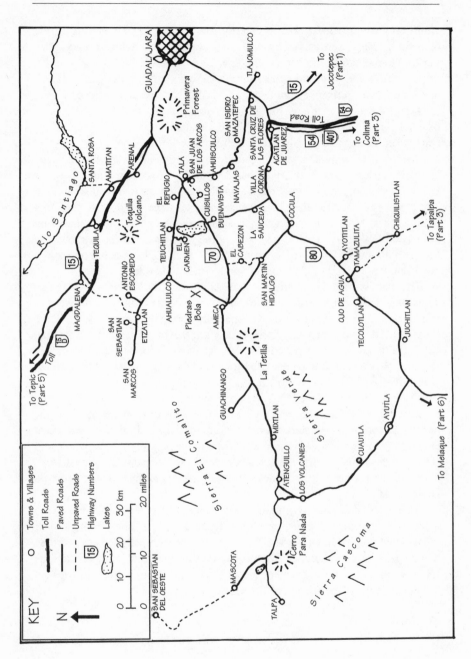

Part Two

9. Highway to the Past
Jalisco's Ex-Hacienda Route

West of Guadalajara is a fascinating area of Jalisco. This was the state's agricultural heartland in the eighteenth and nineteenth centuries when the large colonial land-holdings, the haciendas, reigned supreme. Virtually all villages in the region were formerly haciendas; in many cases, parts of the old buildings can still be seen and explored.

Santa Cruz de las Flores

The starting point for the "Hacienda Highway" is the village of Santa Cruz de las Flores, mid-way between Guadalajara and Jocotepec.

In the centre of this dishevelled and dusty little town are two of Jalisco's most interesting religious buildings, the details of which almost defy description. Indeed, a commentator in 1917 was moved to use the terms "byzantine", "arab", "renaissance", "romantic" and even "gothic" in his attempted description, before finally admitting defeat. These seventeenth century buildings were constructed by local craftsmen, who almost certainly used prints of medieval European churches belonging to their Franciscan converters, in place of conventional architectural plans. The parish church, decorated with flowery motifs, is another particularly fine example of Jaliscan Popular Baroque. The Hospital Chapel has both an unusual shape (see for yourself) and many astronomical symbols in its stonework. Purists argue that both buildings have been badly restored, but don't let that put you off visiting them.

The hacienda route, the road to Tala, leaves Highway 15 by the Pemex gasoline station, and passes first one, then another, ex-hacienda now in ruins. There are too many for a comprehensive list but some of the more outstanding are described here. Even if you're not particularly interested in the history of the various villages, this route is a pretty drive through rolling hills with a variety of pleasant scenery and plenty of photo opportunities.

Mazatepec

The first hacienda to be encountered is in Mazatepec. The central area of the town is north of the road. In one corner of the attractive town plaza are the ancient walls of the hacienda. The Mazatepec hacienda, founded in 1692, was very prosperous by the 1820's when it was rented for $3100 pesos per year, a sum larger than most municipal budgets of the time. The line of tall palm trees still standing in stately array along the street leading to the plaza once adorned the main driveway to the hacienda entrance. Behind the hacienda would have been the formal gardens.

There are stories of buried treasure associated with most haciendas and Mazatepec is no exception. One member of the family which sold Mazatepec in the 1960's says that when the new owners demolished a huge water tank, they discovered secret rooms beneath it. An arched doorway gave access to a tunnel leading to the hacienda's kitchen. The rooms and tunnel must have been built as a hiding place for use in the event of the Great House being attacked by bandits or revolutionaries. No one knows exactly when the rooms were built or precisely what treasures they once contained.

Mazatepec is on the main railway line between Guadalajara and Manzanillo. Passengers can still disembark in Mazatepec, but its lovely mid-century station building was closed to the public in the early 1990's. The railway, with its sidings and signalling system, has seen trains for over a hundred years; it is south of the highway. Between road and track is the Río Escondido (Hidden River) spa, a pleasant place for a day out, with large, clean, thermal pools, playground for children, barbecues and restaurant. It also has bungalows for rent.

Navajas

A tall stand of eucalyptus trees about twenty kilometres from Santa Cruz marks the entrance to Navajas. The narrow access road (rough, dirt) passes the village soccer pitch and conical grain storages before entering the confines of the ex-hacienda. Navajas is an interesting introduction to the subject of former haciendas, not least because a complete inventory of the buildings and grounds exists from more than a hundred and sixty years ago. This inventory formed the basis of the description of a typical nineteenth century hacienda in Lindley (1983). Suffice it to say that Navajas had a 12-room Great House, a chapel, several granaries, a small plaza, a carriage house and two or three corrals, besides the usual workers' cottages, miscellaneous sheds and threshing floors. In its orchard were more than a thousand fruit trees, including peaches, pomegranates, bananas, oranges, figs, avocados, grapefruit, apricots and cherries. Life was lived on a grand scale in those days, provided, of course, you were the hacienda owner or a member of his family. Navajas' outbuildings are now in ruins and the Great House is occupied by several different families, not living in quite such a grand style. They are very friendly and usually allow visitors, on polite request, to look around.

Ahuisculco and San Juan de los Arcos

Another few kilometres along the main road, a lane branches off to the left, leading through Ahuisculco, quite a picturesque little village. Whether or not you take this left-hand fork, you eventually reach San Juan de los Arcos. The arches referred to are tall, stone arches, supporting an ancient aqueduct. Only a few steps off the road is the village plaza, with its church (formerly the hacienda chapel) and the ex-Great House, which had a second floor lookout or mirador, from which to survey the surrounding countryside.

Teuchitlan

Cuisillos

Directly west of San Juan is the very different ex-hacienda of Cuisillos. The straight-line dirt road between the two is usually in good condition; alternatively, continue along the highway to Tala, drive out the other side, turning left on Highway 70, and watch for the Cuisillos sign, again on the left. Either way, in the middle of the forest of thirty-foot television antennas that is Cuisillos, is a tidy, neoclassic church, Our Lady of the Rosary, with bright blue doors and crenellated "battlements" on top. This was the chapel of Cuisillos hacienda, which was a major sugar-producing operation, prior to its break-up.

La Sauceda

By now it's midday and time for something to eat. At the entrance to Teuchitlán (15 kilometres from Highway 70, junction near Tala) are several excellent restaurants. Passing El Refugio and La Estanzuela (both naturally, ex-haciendas) the road descends onto a bridge, with Teuchitlán visible on the right-hand side. Just before the bridge a track to the left provides access to half-a-dozen open-air restaurants. They all serve similar fare. The best choice is the fresh-water fish, plucked only seconds before from the nearby lagoon. The waters of this lagoon, surprise, surprise, lap around the ruins of yet another ex-hacienda out in the middle.

Six kilometres beyond Teuchitlán a dirt road to the left leads to the very attractive and still inhabited hacienda of El Carmen; unfortunately, little of this hacienda is visible from the road. Although this is a private residence of the Baeza family, visitors are often permitted to look around if they first ask permission. Built by Franciscan monks in the late sixteenth century, the Great House is a magnificent two storey building with a beautiful interior patio. The present owners are avid treasure-hunters and have excavated many parts of their property looking for hidden gold and silver.

Buenavista

Another option for the enquiring visitor to hacienda-country is to return to Highway 70 and turn south-west towards Ameca. Ten minutes past the Cuisillos entrance is a crossroads. Turn left to enter Buenavista, a somewhat inappropriate name, since there is no "good view" from anywhere in the village. Lovers of the unexpected will delight in the parish church, around whose courtyard stand larger-than-life size statues of the twelve apostles. Standing guard above the doorway of the church is Moses with his stone tablets. This beautifully restored building dates from 1881 and was the work of Benito Velasco. All the expenses of this project were covered by local *hacendado* (hacienda-owner) Ignacio Cañedo, a member of one of the best known of Guadalajara's oligarchic families. Cañedo was also responsible for the construction of the area's most noteworthy religious building, the chapel of El Cabezón, further west.

El Cabezón

Who would guess, judging by the unprepossessing landscape around El Cabezón, that this was once one of the area's richest haciendas and that a master-piece of nineteenth century religious art is to be found here? But the drive, along an unpaved road, is well worth the effort. The area immediately around the chapel has been repaved, and regularly-spaced trees and a fountain vie for attention in front of the main door. From the outside there is little to suggest the opulence displayed within.

The fine polish of the interior woodwork, all in mesquite, and numerous monuments to members of the Cañedo family, are overshadowed by one of the best preserved gilded altars in Jalisco. The chapel is small enough to be considered informal, large enough to warrant the term glorious. The architect of this religious masterpiece was Francisco Eduardo Tresguerras.

Many of the surrounding buildings date from the same period, but they lie in ruins. The strong faith of the local people has ensured that this particular relic of hacienda times has not been allowed to fall into disrepair. What an impressive place this must have been a hundred years ago.

From El Cabezón, twenty minutes along a reasonably smooth dirt road (ask for directions) is sufficient to reach San Martín de Hidalgo and then Highway 80 near the town of Cocula, birthplace of mariachi music.

La Sauceda

If time and daylight permit, only eight kilometres from Cocula on this return route is a paved road to the magnificent hacienda of La Sauceda. This is a fine example of classical hacienda style, imposing and beautiful. The crucifix in the chapel which probably dates from the sixteenth century was found in the middle of a dense thicket of thorns near the village. It is carried in solemn procession to Cocula and back, every Easter.

The evocative ruins of these ex-haciendas conjure up images of a Mexico unknown to most visitors. At one and the same time they recall the wealth of a relatively small number of families who were the economic pillars of colonial Mexico, as well as the social inequalities which were eventually to result in the turmoil of the Mexican Revolution at the start of this century.

Spas of Villa Corona

The last part of the route, before it joins the Guadalajara-Colima highway, passes through Villa Corona, a town with several warm-water spas. The biggest spa here, Agua Caliente, has superb facilities for entertaining children of any age, with well supervised sports courts, giant waterslides, toboggans, a fully-equipped playground and even a pool where artificial waves delight the youngsters who want to play in surf. Meanwhile, mom and dad can enjoy the quieter delights of huge warm swimming pools and the spa's restaurant-bar. RV travellers will want to spend several nights in Agua Caliente's deservedly popular trailer park.

Villa Corona, named after General Ramón Corona (page 35), houses an extraordinary manifestation of one man's devotion to the Catholic faith. For more than fifty years, J. Jesús Navarro, ably assisted on occasion by his sons, has chipped away at a sandstone hill a few steps from his home, gradually creating one of the most unusual chapels in Mexico. Quarried into a hillside, on the northern edge of the town, is a long, graceful nave, of delightful proportions, dedicated to the Virgin of Lourdes. The lighting, now electric, was originally provided by means of a mirror, used to reflect the sunlight from the courtyard outside. To find the chapel, ask for La Iglesia de Arena (the Church of Sand).

• • •

10. The Towns Around Tequila Volcano

Tala

This loop begins in the sugar factory town of Tala, founded by the Spanish in the early sixteenth century. The town is not particularly attractive though it has an old church, dedicated to San Francisco, originally constructed soon after the town was founded, but extensively rebuilt in later centuries. Tala celebrates its patron saint each year in a lively nine day fiesta with parades, music, dancing and fireworks, ending on October 4th.

From Tala, state Highway 4 goes westwards through Teuchitlán, Ahualulco and Etzatlán, all of which were very important towns in colonial times when this route formed part of the main Guadalajara-Tepic-Pacific coast route. For much of the early part of the drive the summit of Tequila volcano, with its distinctive "spine," is visible to the north. The now more important Tequila-Magdalena route was built two hundred years later and forms a natural return route for this trip.

Teuchitlán

Just before Teuchitlán (excellent fish restaurants, page 59), there are often fishermen showing off their prowess from the small bridge which crosses an arm of the La Vega reservoir. This reservoir, like most others in Mexico, is an excellent bird-watching spot.

Teuchitlán has an abandoned air about it, and the peeling paintwork and crumbling walls around the tree-filled plaza are all that is left of its former glory. A short distance north of the town is a small *balneario* or spa, El Rincón, with luke-warm water, and this same track leads to the archaeological site known as Guachimontón. There is little to be seen here apart from mounds of earth; however, recent research by Phil Weigand is revealing a beautiful, circular – and presumably symbolic – symmetry in the original architecture. Similarities of style have been identified in many other nearby sites.

The scenery throughout this trip is varied and interesting, green sugarcane fields on the flat land contrasting with the forests of the higher slopes, and small lakes and hills leading the eye to distant peaks. Far off the normal tourist trail, the route offers glimpses into everyday Mexico as lived by Mexicans, small villages and busy towns, corn *masa* being ground by hand to make tortillas, wood-smoke curling skywards to one side of cement-block houses and the tempting smell of home-cooked food wafting along on the breeze.

How the Piedras Bola Formed

T he *National Geographic* article (August 1969) was written after a former Superintendent of the Piedra Bola mine, Ernest Gordon, persuaded Matthew Stirling, a renowned archaeologist, and Dr. Robert Smith of the U.S. Geological Survey, to visit the area. Dr. Smith's explanation of the origin of the stone spheres is summarised below:

During the Tertiary geological era, 10-12 million years ago, a local volcano erupted, causing a deluge of glassy fragments of molten lava and ash, together with large quantities of volcanic gas trapped in the mixture. The mixture was very hot, probably between 550 and 800°C. The deluge of material partially filled an existing valley, burying the former surface.

As the mixture cooled down, the existing glassy fragments formed nuclei around which much of the remainder of the material crystallized. Spherical balls began to form, their size depending on how long the crystallization process continued uninterrupted. The longer the time, the bigger the ball....

The most perfect balls were formed near the previous ground level, inside the hot mass of ashes, where the cooling would have occured more evenly than in the bulk of the matrix material. The crystallized material is a kind of rhyolite which has an identical chemical composition to the fragments of glassy obsidian also found in the area.

The remainder of the ashes cooled down and became a consolidated accumulation of ashes and glassy fragments or tuff, without clearly defined spheres. This tuff is weaker, and has a lower density than the stone balls within it.

During succeeding millenia, the combined processes of physical and chemical weathering weakened the surrounding tuff, and water (rain and rivulets) then eroded away this loose material, exposing some of the rhyolitic boulders completely and others partially. As these processes continue, so more of the boulders will be exhumed from beneath their cover of tuff, and be revealed to us.

● ● ●

Piedras Bola

Ahualulco

Ahualulco, next on our route, is also an old Spanish settlement, founded in 1531. The formal name of the town is Ahualulco de Mercado, the Mercado part referring not to the local market but to Father José María Mercado, a native of the town, one of the priests involved on the rebel side in the Mexican War of Independence. In colonial times, Ahualulco was a gold and silver-mining centre.

Ahualulco is the jumping-off point for a full day horseback expedition into the hills, the Sierra of Ameca, south of the road, to explore around the old silver mine of Piedra Bola (Stone Ball) and Agua Blanca. A photograph of this area appeared on the cover of *National Geographic*. In the middle of the forest are more than a hundred and fifty strange stone balls, almost perfectly spherical, ranging in diameter from about sixty centimetres to more than three metres. These symmetrical boulders are unusually large. Nothing quite like them exists elsewhere in Mexico, or, according to current scientific opinion, anywhere else in the world.

Nearby is an area called Las Iglesias (The Churches), which has gothic-looking towers and spires formed by erosion in the sand. A hiking trail to the Piedras Bola and Las Iglesias begins from km. 13 of the paved road that crosses the mountains between Ahualulco and Ameca. Allow several hours for the hike. So that people who don't have time to go exploring the hills can still get some idea of these extraordinary stone spheres, the locals have thoughtfully rolled one down the mountain and onto Ahualulco's plaza.

Etzatlán

Only twenty minutes drive from Ahualulco is Etzatlán. One kilometre west of Etzatlán is the track leading to the ex-hacienda of San Sebastián. Some of the buildings here are occupied by the impoverished families of former workers. The Great House, which must have been magnificent, is in ruins. Close to here, an unusually deep pre-Columbian shaft tomb was discovered, excavated some 16 metres underground in solid rock. The work involved in digging the shaft, two tunnels and three chambers comprising the tomb is mind-boggling, given that the Indians who built it had only stone tools. Items found in the tomb are displayed in the Regional Museum in Guadalajara.

Etzatlán was a major colonial mining centre. Silver was discovered locally in 1540, the same year that work was started on the parish church. Though the origin of its name is unclear, it probably means "place of blood" but exactly whose blood is being remembered in this etymology no one knows. The town lived up to its name in the early years of colonization when the local Indian chief, Coaxicar, ordered the slaughter of the Franciscan priests based here. Today, Etzatlán is a large, bustling town with two of the very few trailer parks which exist in Jalisco.

Magdalena and Its Lake

From the domestic gas depot at the entrance to Etzatlán, a dirt road leads to Magdalena. The route is not well signposted, so ask for directions every time you're in doubt. This road skirts the edge of what was once a large body of water, Magdalena Lake, subsequently drained for agriculture. Of course, when the Franciscans arrived, the lake existed in all its glory. An interesting legend relates what happened when the local non-baptised Indians threw a small sculpture of the crucified Christ, offered them by the priests, into its waters. Far from sinking as the Indians had expected, the sculpture floated clear across to the opposite side, where it was recovered to be duly worshipped by all, Indians and priests alike. The sculpture, known as "Our Lord of the Waters" is now in Guadalajara cathedral.

Magdalena has, unfortunately, suffered the same fate as so many Mexican towns located astride a major highway, becoming a grimy and noisy stopping place for long distance traffic. Its central area would be very attractive if it weren't for the gigantic double trailers trying to negotiate the tight corners without further scraping the ancient walls.

The Spanish discovered, probably to their surprise, that the rocks in the hills around Magdalena contained large quantities of fine opals. Even today, trade in opals is still a major source of income in the town; passers-by may either visit local stores, which prefer to sell cut stones, or haggle with street vendors anxious to prove that their rough opals are superior to everyone else's. Enterprising visitors have often bartered old clothes and shoes for prize opals. Allow plenty of time here if you wish to visit the actual mines since they are some distance from the town. The larger and more accessible mines include San Simeón, famous for harlequin and rain-fire opals, and La Mazata near La Estancia. Magdalena's claim to being

Silver Mining Methods in Colonial Times

T hroughout Spanish colonial times, mine operators had to surrender as much as one fifth of all the silver mined to the Crown. In the early days, the ore was extracted by men and boys climbing down notched tree-trunk ladders holding candles. Since most Mexican ore was high in sulphides, it was enriched using a method invented in Pachuca, Mexico, in the 1550's: amalgamation by mercury. This was a cost-effecive process fundamental to Spanish colonial power, which used no water-power, no skilled workmen, and no machinery. Spain's monopoly on many parts of the process resulted in a thriving black market for illicitly-produced silver.

Once mined, the ore was ground into a fine powder in a series of stone drag mills operated by mules or horses. This took place in the *hacienda de beneficio* (the enrichment works). The powder was mixed with water, then dumped on the flagstone *patio*, and spread into circular mounds (*tortas*), about 30 metres in diameter, to drain.

Then the *azoguero* (mercury-man) took charge – using sight, touch and smell, he added doses of salt and copper sulphate to the tortas, and left them to "cook" for a few days. Next he sprinkled mercury on top, which was trodden in; the mixture was left for between one and six months, depending on ore quality and weather. This decomposed the silver sulphide, forming silver chloride, which in turn was absorbed by the mercury. Until 1784, men and boys did the mixing, often absorbing enough mercury to result in lower limb paralysis, and even death.

The amalgam of mercury and silver was allowed to settle out, collected into cloth sacks and pressed to extract any surplus mercury – this was too expensive to waste. The silver was then recovered from the amalgam by heating. About 15 ounces of silver were obtained per ton of ore. This basic process, the patio process, continued unchanged into the twentieth century.

Based on Todd (1977)

• • •

Tequila Volcano

the opal capital of Mexico is hotly disputed by San Juan del Río in the state of Querétaro, which claims the same distinction. From Magdalena, allow about 90 minutes driving time back to Guadalajara via Tequila and Amatitán.

Tequila – Not Just a Drink

Lovers of curiosities will find plenty to whet their appetite and satisfy their thirst in the small town of Tequila. The town lies in the shadow of an imposing 2700-metre (8860-foot) volcano, which has the distinction of being drive-in by virtue of a cobblestone road built for access to the short-wave communications tower located on its rim.

The seventeen kilometre drive from the town centre, past the small wild west railway station, to the top of the volcano provides glorious views over the surrounding countryside, and an opportunity, for the biologically-curious, to witness the rapid changes of flora that occur with increasing altitude. Look particularly for different species of oak trees including the black or emory oak with its edible acorns, and for bromeliads growing on the trees. The ascent is also a delight for bird-watchers with good odds on seeing as many as 60 different species in a single day.

From the end of the road it is but a short walk to the rim of the crater. Here, without question, the most arresting thing about the view is not the crater, tree-lined and green though it is, but the giant monolith with almost vertical sides rising perpendicularly from the middle of the crater floor. This well-preserved central spine is extremely unusual – and, for the geologically-curious, most likely represents the hardened lava which cooled in the central vent of the volcano and which, solid and unyielding, was pushed upwards at a later date by tremendous subterranean pressure. Few such good examples exist anywhere in the world.

Looking across the crater, on a day when clouds drift overhead and partially obscure the view, is like watching a modern day video equivalent of ancient Chinese landscape drawings.

There is plenty of material here, too, for the historically-curious. They will discover that the town dates from soon after the arrival of the Spanish conquistadores, led by the barbarous Nuño Beltran de Guzmán. Its name supposedly derives from "place of tricks" or "place of those who pay tribute".

During Mexico's War of Independence (1810-21), Tequila gained increased prosperity, partly because communications between Guadalajara, then the capital of New Galicia, and Mexico City, the capital of New Spain, were severed. Tequila lay on the route west from Guadalajara to the port of San Blas. In 1812, the Royalist Governor, José de la Cruz, managed to chase off the rebel insurgents and reopen the port of San Blas for business. This allowed merchants from England, France, the U.S. and Panama to arrive and trade – they did, and Guadalajara and Tequila prospered. Many famous tequila brands date from this period.

Sixty years later, Manuel Lozada, "The Tiger of Alica", proclaimed a plan for

The Production of Tequila

T equila is made from agave plants, which are no relation botanically to cacti, even though they are often mistakenly associated with them. Agaves are commonly called "century plants" in the U.S.A., a name derived from the length of time they grow before producing a flowering stalk – actually, from eight to twenty years depending on the species, rather than the hundred suggested by their common name. Some species flower only once and die shortly afterwards, others can flower almost every year.

The tequila agaves are started from seed or from onion-size cuttings. When the plants are mature (6 to 12 years later), their branches are cut off, using a long-handled knife called a *coa*, leaving the *cabeza* (or "pineapple"), which is the part used for juice extraction. Cabezas (which weigh from 10 to 120 kilos) are cut in half, and then baked in stone furnaces or stainless steel autoclaves for one to three days to convert their starches into sugars.

From the ovens, the now golden-brown cabezas are shredded and placed in mills which extract the juices or *mosto*. The mixture is allowed to ferment for several days, then two distillations are performed to extract the almost colourless white or silver tequila. The spirit's taste depends principally on the length of fermentation. Golden (*añejo*) or amber (*reposado*) tequila results from storage in ex brandy or wine casks made of white oak for between one and six months.

• • •

liberating the western part of Jalisco and placed thousands of indigenous people on a war footing; he advanced towards Guadalajara, calling for the overthrow of the state government. On January 24th, 1873, he took the town of Tequila, but only after stubborn resistance from the politician Sixto Gorjón, 50 police and a few neighbours. This heroic resistance led to Tequila being named a city on January 9th,1874.

"Appelacion Controlée"

Though colonial authorities tried to suppress illegal liquors, the industry of illicit distilling clearly thrived. One eighteenth century source lists more than 81 different mixtures, including some truly fearsome-sounding concoctions such as "cock's eye", "rabbit's blood", "bone-breaker" and "excommunication". By the 1670's, the authorities saw the wisdom of taxing, rather than prohibiting, liquor production.

For centuries, distilled agave juice was known as *mezcal*. As far as we know, a Spanish medic, Gerónimo Hernández, was the first foreigner to sample it, in the year 1651. The original method for producing mezcal used clay ovens and pots.

By the end of the nineteenth century, as the railroads expanded, the reputation of Tequila spread further afield; this is when the *vino de mezcal* produced in Tequila became so popular that people began calling it simply "tequila", and it was adopted as Mexico's national drink.

To qualify as genuine tequila, the drink has to be manufactured in the state of Jalisco or in certain areas along the state line. An estimated 100 million maguey plants are cultivated on approximately 40,000 hectares. More than 50 million litres of tequila are produced each year. About 40% of this quantity is exported.

Connoisseurs argue long and loud as to which is the better product, but all agree that the only tequila made from 100% *Agave tequilana Weber azul,* the ultimate

The Filipino Connection

P re-Columbian Indians knew how to produce several different drinks from agave plants, but their techniques did not include distillation, and hence, strictly speaking, they did not produce tequila. Fermented agave juice or *pulque* may be the oldest alcoholic drink on the continent; it is referred to in an archival Olmec text which claims that it serves as a "delight for the gods and priests". Pulque was fermented, but not distilled.

If the pre-Columbians didn't have distilled agave drinks, then how, when and where did distillation of agave first occur? In 1897, Carl Lumholtz, the famous Norwegian ethnologist, who spent several years living with remote Indian tribes in Mexico, found that the Huichol Indians in eastern Nayarit distilled agave juice using simple stills, but with pots which seemed to be quite unlike anything Spanish or pre-Columbian in origin.

By 1944, Henry Bruman, a University of California geographer, had documented how Filipino seamen on the Manila Galleon had brought similar stills to western Mexico, for making coconut brandy, during the late sixteenth century.

Dr. Nyle Walton, of the University of Florida, expanded on Bruman's work, showing how the Spanish authorities had sought to suppress Mexican liquor production because it threatened to compete with Spanish brandy. This suppression led to the establishment of illicit distilling in many remote areas including parts of Colima and Jalisco. Even today, the word "tuba", which means "coconut wine" in the Filipino Tagalog language, is used in Jalisco for mezcal wine before it is distilled for tequila. This is probably because the first stills used for mezcal distillation were Filipino in origin.

• • •

in quality, is Tequila Herradura, manufactured in Amatitán, a town between Tequila and Guadalajara. Anyone interested in the history of tequila will enjoy a visit to Herradura's old hacienda "San José del Refugio" in Amatitán; tequila is made here just as in the early days. The factory is a working museum with mule-operated mills, and primitive distillation ovens, fuelled by the bagasse of the maguey. The Great House is classic in style, with a wide entrance stairway and a first floor balustrade the full width of the building.

Amatitán is also worth visiting, in order to see one of Jalisco's hydro-electric power stations. The Santa Rosa plant is on the River Santiago, only 14 kilometres north of Amatitán, and the short drive affords excellent scenic views.

Today, visitors to the town of Tequila can not only enter any one of several tequila factories to watch the processing and taste a sample but can also admire one of the few public monuments to liquor anywhere in the world – a fountain which has water emerging from a stone bottle supported in an agave plant.

Any time of year is good for a visit but, if you can, why not try to sample the town and its famous beverage in the first half of December during the annual Tequila fair or on May 13th, official Tequila Day?

Next time you say "¡Salud!" with a margarita in your hand, spare a thought for the poor pre-Columbians who may have known of Tequila the volcano, but who lived in ignorance of the delights of tequila the drink, now produced on the volcano's slopes.

The Primavera Forest

However, the Indians certainly didn't live in ignorance of the value of another volcanic product, obsidian. Some of the largest deposits of obsidian in all of Mexico lie just south of the highway between Tequila and Guadalajara in the Primavera Forest, a wilderness area of pines and oaks, which also boasts hot rivers, nature-trails and thermal spas. Huge blocks of this glassy, black rock litter the roadsides. The rock formed when blocks of hot lava, still molten, rained into the cold waters of a lake, cooling instantaneously. It was in great demand among the Indians for the manufacture of arrow-heads and knives.

• • •

11. Talpa and Mascota
Mountains and Miracles

West of Ameca, a modern scenic highway with fine views of beautiful valleys and rugged mountain ranges leads to Talpa, one of Jalisco's major religious centres. Beyond the Talpa-Mascota junction, a soon-to-be-paved road continues northwards through Mascota and San Sebastian del Oeste, eventually descending from the sierras into the outskirts of Puerto Vallarta, the Pacific jet-set resort made famous by Richard Burton and Elizabeth Taylor. Once complete, this route will considerably shorten the time required to drive from Guadalajara to Puerto Vallarta.

Already, Highway 70 has brought Talpa, formerly reached only after a gruelling ten hour marathon on snaking mountain roads, within easy reach of the Guadalajara and Lake Chapala areas, making it an excellent choice for an interesting overnight trip.

From Ameca the first stage of the route is a leisurely climb through the rolling, scrub-covered foothills of the majestic volcanic peak of La Tetilla (The Tit). This is the start of gold country. Eight kilometres north of the highway is the prosperous small mining town of Guachinango. The road providing access to the town cuts through richly-veined rocks of many hues: red, coppery green, grey, brown and yellow. The same colours give the town's main church a distinctive look. On close examination, its exterior proves to be decorated with a dazzling selection of small pieces of unmatched ceramic tiles. Here and there an entire tea-plate is embedded in the cement. The effect is extraordinary.

Guachinango is a seductively attractive town. Its friendly inhabitants are happy to encourage you in peering through doorways or in watching the local baker delicately remove long planks loaded with freshly-baked *pan dulce* (sweet breads) from the glowing embers of his hot oven.

The main road continues westwards and the scenery becomes ever more impressive. The area between Mixtlán ("place of clouds") and Atenguillo is ranching and corn-growing country. Beyond Atenguillo the road winds steeply, gaining more than five hundred metres in height in a few kilometres before joining the Mascota-Ayutla road, Highway 35. There are spectacular views to the south along this section and several pull-off places to stretch your legs and take a photo.

This road junction is about fifty minutes from Talpa. Eroded rocks visible on distant hillsides resemble animals' heads but have no formal names. The prominent hill south of the road is called Cerro Para Nada. Who knows what prompted this strange name, which literally means "hill for nothing" or "hill? no way!"

A few kilometres outside Talpa is a chapel on the right-hand side and a large parking area. Pull off the road and climb the few steps of La Cruz de Romero to admire the view over the town and valley far below. The original cross was erected by José Romero, a Talpa architect who built the town hall. It was replaced by his nephew after being worn out by the incessant kisses of passing pilgrims, thankful to have reached this promontory overlooking their destination. Before driving off again, check your brakes since the descent to the town is by one of the steepest paved roads anywhere in Mexico. A toll is levied on visitors who successfully arrive at the bottom still in one piece, to ensure that the many hairpin bends along this road can be adequately maintained.

Despite its location in the bottom of a valley, the name Talpa is supposed to mean "high place." Whether or not you believe that, as you walk around the town it quickly becomes obvious that this is a major religious centre. The signs are everywhere, from the small stalls selling candles, prayer guides and rosaries to the shops which sell "everything for the pilgrim", from the number of churches to the monumental statue of Christ the King which overlooks and protects the town from its elevated position on the nearest hill. It is worth climbing up to the Cristo Rey if only for the view.

Talpa has been a place of pilgrimage for several hundred years. The most venerated statue is that of Nuestra Señora del Rosario. Made of sugar-cane paste by a Tarascan Indian in Los Reyes, Michoacán in the 1530's, it was brought to Talpa in 1585, fourteen years before the town was officially founded. In 1644 the statue, then housed in the San José church, one block from the main plaza, was in a poor state of repair and due for replacement. In a story echoed in the miraculous happenings in another religious centre, San Juan de los Lagos (chapter 16), as the statue was being taken down on the 19th of September, it suddenly emitted a bright light, dazzling all the onlookers present. When their sight returned, they discovered, to their amazement, that the Virgin was as good as new. This miracle caused the townspeople to erect a special sanctuary for the statue, which they completed in 1651. The present sanctuary, a minor basilica, dates from 1755.

In 1660 the statue was taken to the nearby town of Mascota during an epidemic and succeeded in immediately abating both the plague and its resultant heavy death-toll. The miracles continued and the statue is visited by thousands of her faithful followers each year, especially during her main fiesta from the 10th to the 19th of September. On the first day, after a procession over a colourful, patterned carpet of sawdust and wildflowers, the Virgin is given a ceremonial wash and a change of clothes. For each of the next nine days the town echoes to the sounds of bells, firecrackers, music and merrymaking, the early morning mists look and smell like incense and the streets are littered with confetti.

The town celebrates other days, too, including Candlemas on February 2nd, the Fair of San José on March 19th, the Coronation on May 12th, and Guadalupe Day, December 12th.

As you stroll through the narrow streets of Talpa, vendors, young and old but invariably friendly and polite, will try to persuade you to buy their guava-flavoured candy, which you can see being made in huge copper vats in several local shops, or to purchase colourful and highly realistic-looking miniature flowers and fruit baskets made of chicle, chewing gum. These look much too good to eat – better to buy them as unusual and inexpensive gifts.

The Talpa region has long been renowned for its chicle. Pre-Columbian Indians used the sticky latex of the sapotaceous trees native to this area to make hard, rubber-like balls. During the Second World War, considerable quantities of chicle were exported to the U.S. Handmade chicle figures are prized collectors' items. A particularly fine model of an entire village *paseo* (page 29), with dozens of incredibly-detailed chicle figures, can be seen in the Guadalajara Regional Museum.

Talpa's town hall is a lovely colonial building dating from 1802. Inside, a mural by Santiago Rosas Zepeda depicts the defense of the plaza when the town was attacked by two hundred followers of Carranza, in the middle of the Mexican Revolution.

For much of the nineteenth century, Talpa was an important gold and silver mining centre. A chalice of pure gold, made in Talpa and intended as a gift to the Vatican, mysteriously ended up instead in the Mexico City cathedral.

If you want to visit Mascota, twenty five kilometres north of Talpa, allow plenty of time since half the distance is still unpaved. It is a beautiful drive past an attractive lake, interesting rock formations and plenty of pine trees.

Mascota is bigger than Talpa and has many lovely, solid-looking stone buildings, though none of them is more than 150 years old, since in 1860 the military commander Antonio Rojas, "The Nero of Jalisco", set fire to the town and razed it to the ground in a fit of pique. The massive, evocative ruins of an eight-eenth century church, which was never completed, are a few blocks north of the plaza. What was originally a side chapel of this church is now used by the well-maintained seminary next door.

Drivers of vehicles with high clearance, seeking a challenge, will enjoy the

road beyond Mascota to San Sebastian del Oeste, a former mining town which in its heyday had 20,000 inhabitants. Mining operations were severely curtailed after a miners' strike in 1888 and today San Sebastian, a character-full ghost town with its own small hotel, is a popular destination for jeep, horseback and light aircraft trips from Puerto Vallarta.

Talpa and Mascota can also be easily reached from the main Guadalajara-Melaque highway by taking Highway 35 through Ayutla and Cuautla. This, of course, makes Talpa very accessible from both Manzanillo and Barra de Navidad on the coast.

On the Las Aguilas hilltop south of Cuautla are intriguing rock formations, of uncertain origin, which have been dubbed Mexico's "Stonehenge". Three great vertical rocks, standing side by side, channel the first rays of the rising sun on equinox and solstice days onto smaller, apparently hand-hewn, marker stones half-buried in the ground. Dozens of large, rounded rocks in the vicinity have hollowed-out centres which may once have had wooden poles inserted in them making additional markers or measuring devices. It is easy to find obsidian arrow-heads and fragments of reddish-coloured earthenware vessels in this area; unfortunately, treasure-hunters seeking buried gold and silver may have inadvertently destroyed most evidence for the precise functions of this pre-Columbian astronomical observatory.

The people in this region have many legends and stories to relate besides those associated with their ancestral astronomers of Las Aguilas. The older inhabitants of Cuautla tell how the first settlement in this area came to nought when a cholera epidemic ravaged the village of Tetitlán, forcing its complete abandonment. People in nearby Ayutla live in fear and trembling of the large volcanic monolith known as La Tortuga (The Turtle), which overshadows the town. The hill is held responsible for enticing young shepherd boys away from their flocks. Some of them have disappeared beneath the hill, Pied Piper fashon, never to be seen again in the outside world. And why should they, when the city beneath the hill is said to have diamond-studded streets and palaces built of pure gold ? Ayutla is only ten minutes drive from Highway 80, two hours from Guadalajara.

If time permits, stop in Tecolotlán, find the plaza, and have a quick look at the fossilized remains of a giant turtle, more than 35,000 years old, in the town's small museum. A few kilometres north, at Ojo del Agua, is the side-road to Tamazulita, an exceptionally pretty and photogenic little village of single-storey adobe buildings on narrow, winding cobblestone streets; it can justifiably be considered the "Taxco" of Jalisco. Either the graded dirt road from here, or the modern paved road which leaves the main highway three kilometres nearer Guadalajara, will take you to Chiquilistlán. From this latter town, an unpaved road winds and bumps its way through mountain scenery of incomparable beauty to Tapalpa (chapter 12). This is truly one of the undiscovered scenic spectaculars of Western Mexico.

• • •

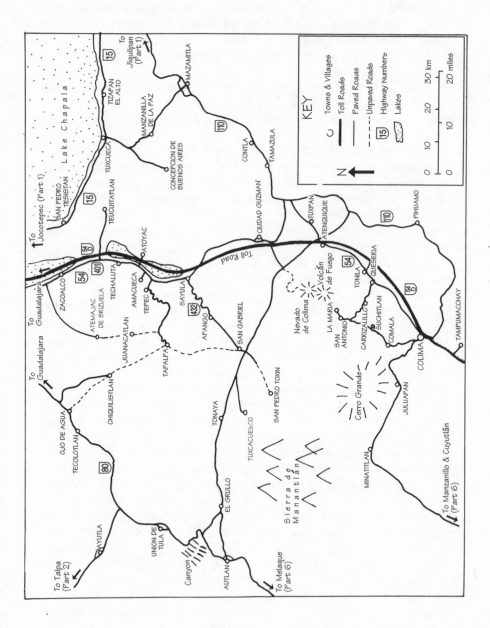

Part Three

12. Tapalpa
A Picturesque Mountain Town

Tapalpa is a favourite destination for city dwellers looking for a change of
pace. The two and a half hours drive from Guadalajara or Chapala passes
through fine and varied scenery and the suggested route includes several small
villages, each with its own fascinating history.

The old road leaves the modern Guadalajara-Colima super-highway just
before the first toll station and then winds downhill past Acatlán de Juárez.

"Acatlán de Juárez" is a typical compound, post-conquest place name, combining the elements, *acatl* (= sugar-cane, introduced into Mexico by the Spanish),
tlan (= in) and Juárez, the leader of the Mexican Reform movement in the mid
nineteenth century. The town's associations with Juárez date from the 20th March,
1858, when Juárez, who had narrowly avoided an assassination attempt a few days
earlier in Guadalajara's Government Palace, gave a speech in Acatlán in which he
praised all the people of Jalisco, saying that "For its courage and freedom, Jalisco
is a sacred land", a statement of which all Jaliscans are justifiably proud. There is
an abandoned hacienda in the heart of Acatlán and a great sea of sugar-cane still
surrounds the town.

Zacoalco de Torres comes next. This generally unattractive town has, two
blocks west of its plaza, a lovely Franciscan chapel which dates from 1550. The
town is a major manufacturing centre of *equipal* furniture, the ever-popular,
uniquely Mexican, leather and wood chairs, sofas and tables. One neighbourhood,
the amusingly named Barrio de las Cebollas (Onion Quarter), is responsible for
virtually all the production. The "de Torres" part of Zacoalco's name refers to the
much respected independence fighter, José Antonio Torres. A major battle was
fought near Zacoalco during the War of Independence.

On the higher ground above the "dry" lakes occupying the flat valley floor are

Salt Extraction – Pre-Hispanic Style

The pre-Hispanic salt workers used an ingenious method to extract the salt they required. They filled earthenware vessels of varied form, including bottles, figurines and animals, with water from the lake and allowed the water to evaporate, leaving behind the salt, whereupon they refilled the vessel and waited again, and so on. Once their vessels were full of salt, their only problem was to extract it – they simply smashed the vessels and picked up the salt. Smashed pieces of these vessels, which were called *tepelcates,*   are easy to find even today .

• • •

the villages of Techaluta, Amacueca and Atoyac. Some of these dry lakes have a thin veneer of water, a few centimetres deep, covering them after the rainy season and are home to a very wide variety of aquatic, migratory birdlife. Techaluta is known for scrumptious *pitayas,*   the multi-coloured fruit of a prickly-pear cactus, and Amacueca for excellent nuts, as well as a superb early colonial Franciscan church and convent.

Atoyac, on the far, eastern, side of the valley, was the site of an ancient salt market. Every five days, salt was bartered for other items here and then transported as far away as Mexico City. The salt came, of course, from the shallow, drying up lakes, which have no natural outlet. Even before the Spanish arrived, this area was producing large quantities of the valuable commodity.

At various sites, graves have been found in which the skeletons are accompanied by obsidian arrow heads dating from the period when Tarascan, Colima and Sayula Indians were all disputing the use of the salt lakes. By 1510, the Chief of the Sayula Indians, Cuantoma, held possession of the lakes but was fully occupied fighting off a challenge from the King of the Tarascans, Tangáxoan II. Cuantoma lost a battle at Acatlán, and was on the point of surrender when the King of Colimán (now Colima), came along and defeated both of them. In 1521, the Spanish arrived and took the lot.

A few kilometres before Sayula, a well-paved road, signposted "Tapalpa", climbs to the foot of the steep, faulted scarp that forms the western side of the valley. Part-way up this slope is the entrance to Tepec, a small village best known for its delicious peaches. On the side of one of Tepec's narrow streets are several huge rocks covered with pre-Hispanic petroglyphs. Beyond Tepec, the road climbs steeply offering ever-improving views of the irrigated valley floor far below, and ranges of mountains as far away as the Colima volcanoes. Much of the wild and inhospitable area north of here was scoured for minerals by Spanish prospectors but they failed to find the riches they sought.

At the top of the scarp, the road meanders through pine forests and open meadows that in autumn become an artist's paradise, carpeted with a spectacular array of orange, blue, white and purple wildflowers.

A small crossroads marks the as yet unpaved side road to Juanacatlán, site of an unusual July festival. In 1642, so the story goes, the locals walked to Mexico City to complain to the religious authorities about something. They were presented with a small statue of the Virgin Mary which they dutifully carried back to the town, discovering on their arrival that their problem had been miraculously solved. Nearby villages, learning of this success, asked to "borrow the Virgin". Eventually, she was in such demand that a replica had to be made. Since 1881, on the 17th of July each year, the real Virgin is taken in procession to a nearby spring where the "fiesta to wash the clothes used in the year by Our Lady" is celebrated, with much music and merrymaking.

Suddenly, round a bend, and the town of Tapalpa comes into view with a large lake in the distance. Largely because of the strict enforcement of building regulations which mandate tiled roofs, wooden doors, windows wider than they are tall and so on, Tapalpa retains a picture-book appearance, despite rapid growth in the past few decades. It has been discovered by rich *Tapatíos* (people from Guadalajara) seeking weekend homes, by artists in search of a relaxing yet creative atmosphere (and some very fine artists now live year-round in the town) and by day-trippers who come to enjoy the cool mountain air and to purchase the delicious fresh cheese, cream and home made preserves. Though discovered, it has not been in any way spoiled. Surrounded by attractive scenery, its people remain friendly, its festivals authentic, and its pace unhurried.

Cobblestone streets with numerous steps and arcades make for a delightful central plaza. The only ugly building is the modern twentieth century red-brick church, which replaced the Franciscan parish church of San Antonio, built about 1700, but severely damaged by earthquakes. The old church still stands but needs extensive restoration.

Half a block from the plaza is the local library, named after a Tapalpa-born engineer, Bracamontes, who occupied several government positions in a distinguished career as a public servant. The library is a model of all that a municipal library can and should be, and besides having an extensive book and magazine collection, it houses a large scale relief model of the Tapalpa region and a colourful mural depicting the town's history.

A nearby street, Raul Quintero, is named in honour of the town's best known poet, who began a long poem describing his native town with the suitably descriptive line, "The pine, the laurel and the oak, the flowery fields are yours, O Tapalpa!"

To the south of the town are the waterfalls known as the Salto del Nogal,

Las Piedrotas

Walnut Falls. There are two falls, one of about 10 metres and the other of more than 60 metres height. They are reached via the unpaved La Frontera-Lagunillas road and a fair hike. Only try this with your own vehicle if it has good ground clearance.

A shorter distance on the other side of town is an interesting outcrop of unusual rock formations, much prized as a picnic area. Las Piedras are huge volcanic boulders set in a broad meadow, overlooking a small, meandering stream. Nature-lovers visiting this open area will want to look for the tanagers and flycatchers often found in the vicinity and examine the lichens and cacti which have somehow found a foothold on the boulders. The Piedras are about seven kilometres along the unpaved road to Chiquilistlán, which eventually joins highway 80, the Guadalajara-Melaque road, near the pretty little town of Tamazulita.

Between the Piedras and Tapalpa are the ruins of a nineteenth century paper-mill, the first in Western Mexico, built with English capital. It produced cigarette papers and security paper for banknotes but remained in operation only until 1909.

Back in Tapalpa's plaza, the adventurous should try the local *granada* (pomegranate) punch, served with no pretensions in the bar on the south-east corner. Of the many restaurants, I like the excellent Mexican home-cooking at Paulino's, which overlooks the plaza. Several small hotels can accommodate those who wish to spend more time here. The classiest central hostelry is La Casa de Maty, a truly rare find in a town of this size. Further afield, on the road towards San Gabriel, is the Tapalpa Country Club hotel, complete with tennis courts and a challenging, hillside, nine-hole golf course.

Tapalpa is one of several Jaliscan towns which celebrates the Virgin of Guadalupe not on December 12th, as does most of Mexico, but exactly one month later, on January 12th. This custom began when the townspeople realised that all the best bands were already engaged elsewhere every December – to guarantee good music, they therefore transferred their celebrations to January. To stand in the cool night air and see the parade on January 12th, its entire route lit by smoky bonfires, is really to witness an authentic tradition.

The return route can include Sayula, birthplace of Juan Rulfo, Mexico's most famous novelist. Rulfo, who died in 1986, is best remembered for his novel, "Pedro Páramo" and his collection of short stories, "The Burning Plain and Other Stories", both readily available in excellent English translations. His friends unkindly claimed that if he hadn't sobered up after writing his much-acclaimed works, he would surely have won the Nobel prize for Literature.

Sayula became the major trading station for this extensive valley after Zacoalco had been depopulated by epidemics and slave trafficking in the early seventeenth century. By the mid-nineteenth century, Sayula was particularly famous for its ceramic tiles; indeed, the yellowish tiles on the spires of Guadalajara Cathedral come from here. The town lost its importance after being bypassed by the Guadalajara-Colima railway in 1905.

A few kilometres outside Sayula the road sweeps past an old hacienda, whose chapel sits in splendid isolation atop a steep-sided hill, before rejoining the toll highway which crosses the middle of the "dry" lakes, back to the Acatlán toll booth.

• • •

Wild maize at Manantlán

13. Manantlán Biosphere Reserve
An Ecotourist Wonderland

C ombining serious research with a keen sense of public relations, the Manantlán Biosphere Reserve up in the hills near Autlán permits visitors the unusual chance to experience the astonishing diversity of plant and animal life found in cloud forest, one of the rarest types of vegetation anywhere in the world.

Cloud forest is found only at high altitudes and within the tropics, and its amazing diversity is due to the intermingling of both tropical and temperate species. Next to an imposing oak tree with crinkled, crackling leaves you may find a species of the *Melastomataceae* family with thick, rounded, indubitably tropical leaves. Not surprisingly, cloud forest harbours dozens of animal species including many which are endangered.

Manantlán still doesn't appear in the guidebooks, and, a generation ago, it was probably true to say that nobody was very bothered whether it was a conservation area or not. However, all that changed in 1977 when a young Guadalajara University student, Rafael Guzmán, began looking in the Sierra of Manantlán for an "extinct" grass species, an ancestor of maize, called *Zea perennis*. His search was part of the Flora of Jalisco project of the University's Botanical Institute, and was inspired by, of all things, a drawing on a Christmas card sent by Dr. Hugh Iltis of the University of Wisconsin.

Guzmán's search led not only to the rediscovery of *Zea perennis* but, more importantly, to the much more astonishing discovery of another early version of maize, *Zea diploperennis*. This latter insignificant looking grass may eventually revolutionize world maize production. It is diploid and is the only wild corn resistant or immune to seven of the most common viral diseases which affect commercially grown corn. Apparently it can easily be hybridized with commercial corn since it has the same number of chromosomes. Besides being adapted to high altitude and wet conditions, it is perennial, growing and regrowing from rhizomes as well as seeds. This, of course, makes it a potential gold mine if it can be cultivated successfully. As a front page article in *The New York Times* in 1982 pointed out, it could save millions of dollars annually – the millions of dollars spent on seed, fuel consumption, labour, and in combating soil erosion and viral diseases.

Furthermore, as conservationists are quick to point out, it is important to conserve the genetic diversity found on the planet. To this end, the University of Guadalajara, with both national and international support, successfully applied for Biosphere Reserve status for the 140,000 hectares of the Sierra Manantlán where the discovery was made. Ironically, since the reserve was designated, even larger stands of *Zea diploperennis* have been discovered outside the boundaries of the reserve.

Why is There Such an Astonishing Variety of Flora Here?

The major control within Western Mexico as far as temperatures are concerned is altitude, and a simple relationship exists between a place's altitude and its seasonal temperature highs and lows. Altitude also directly affects rainfall amounts and seasonality.

The large altitude differences found within short distances at many points of the Volcanic Axis means that there is a mosaic of climatic and hence natural vegetation regions including such diverse elements as cloud-forest, tropical deciduous forest, mangrove swamp and pine-oak forest among others.

The position of the Volcanic Axis, along latitude 19°N, and hence well within the tropics, together with Mexico's geological history as a land bridge between continents, further enriches the diversity of species found within it. Mexico has representative areas of virtually all the world's biomes. It is estimated that it has more than 30,000 species of flowering plants, many as yet unidentified, and over 3000 species of vertebrates. The country encompasses the zone of transition between the nearctic and neotropical biogeographical regions (Rzedowski 1978).

Unfortunately, Western Mexico has comparatively little natural vegetation left. Human pressures arising from urbanization and overexploitation of natural resources have severely depleted the areas of truly natural vegetation, which are now largely confined to inaccessible regions.

• • •

Over 2600 species of flowering plants and ferns have been reported to date for the reserve, and many of them, including a previously unknown species of poplar, are endemic to this area. The reserve's fauna includes 333 species of birds (about 30% of Mexico's total number of bird species), 76 mammals (16% Mexican total), 54 reptile species, 20 amphibians and 16 fishes. A previously unknown beetle species has already been found and documented.

Among the more useful animals is a species of wild turkey, *Penelope purpurascens,* one of two endemic Mexican species, a forerunner of many domesticated turkey breeds. The wild turkey is a distinctively heavy bird, a poor flyer, but with strong legs adapted to running and burrowing. It is virtually extinct. Another important animal, also in grave danger of extinction, is the mountain lion or jaguar, *Felis onca.* Several sightings of this and four of the other five Mexican members of the wild cat family have been reported inside the reserve.

A visit to this extraordinary part of southern Jalisco is not without its trials. By contacting the University of Guadalajara, permission can be obtained, and arrangements made, for the very bumpy, four-wheel-drive-only transfer from either Autlán, which has a good range of hotel accommodations, or El Grullo, where the University Research Station offices are, to the Research Station proper in Manantlán. The drive takes about three hours, depending on weather and road conditions. Sometimes only mule or Shanks's pony can make it. The Station has simple bunk-bed accommodation, limited solar-powered electricity and no running water, but any inconvenience is quickly forgotten once visitors arrive into this mountain paradise and taste the Station cook's hand-made tortillas. Manantlán is a magical place. The sounds of the forest are everywhere, and the stars at night incomparable.

The University has laid out two nature trails to ensure that visitors can see the maximum variety of plant and animal life without disturbing the many research programmes being conducted in the zone. The shorter trail (two kilometres, or just over one mile, long) is called Xilosuchitlan, the name of a nearby valley which means "place where the tender corn grows", a possible pre-Columbian reference to perennial maize.

The trail includes stops to appreciate secondary vegetation, which regrew after an area was cleared for agriculture and subsequently abandoned, areas of perennial maize, cloud forest and clearings within it, and an area known as the Hanging Garden where a profusion of climbers, creepers, vines and epiphytes combine to create a luxuriant curtain of greenery.

Only 0.5% of Mexico is this type of forest, and this area is ever-decreasing due to logging, agriculture, cattle-raising and urbanization, as well as due to natural and man-made fires.

The Manantlán reserve, known formally as the Instituto Manantlán de Ecología y Conservación de la Biodiversidad, is supported by numerous national and international organizations, including The Worldwide Fund for Nature, and The Nature Conservancy. Why not add your support, either by visiting this unique area, or by making a donation to the research station's running costs?

For further information, contact the University of Guadalajara's research station office by writing to The Director, IMECBIO, Apartado Postal 69, Autlán, C. P. 48900, Jalisco.

• • •

14. Mazamitla and Tamazula
From Pine Forests to Sugarcane

Mazamitla – A Gem in the Mountains

One of the prettiest towns in Jalisco is Mazamitla, set high in the pine-clad mountains near the Michoacán border. It is a graceful, charming town of cobblestone streets, adobe walls, wooden balconies, old doorways and red-tile roofs. Among its many attractions are the fresh air and scenic beauty of the surrounding countryside, some fine restaurants specialising in Mexican food, and the chance to shop for fresh cream, cheese and home-made preserves. As befits a mountain town, its inhabitants also make lovely woollen sweaters and ponchos, for sale in the local shops.

Mazamitla, a very old town, dates back at least as far as the twelfth century. In 1485, shortly before the Spanish arrived to colonise "New Spain", invading Tarascan Indians from Tzintzuntzan on the shore of Lake Pátzcuaro, successfully gained control of the area around Mazamitla. They then extended their empire even further west to the seasonally dry lakebeds of Sayula and San Marcos, which they wanted for their salt. The Tarascans did not control Mazamitla for long, however; at the conclusion of the "Salt Wars" in 1510, they withdrew.

The Spanish grew to both love and hate Mazamitla. It provided a convenient route for them between the important colonial centre of Valladolid (today called Morelia) and the Colima coast. The town was situated at the highest point (2200 metres or 7300 feet) along this route and was a welcome rest-stop for horses and men who had been forced to ascend steeply just before entering the town.

But during the Mexican struggle for independence (1810-21) it also became a haven for rebel forces intent on breaking the Spanish domination of the country. A few miles outside the town, towards Tamazula, is the site of the Battle of Zapatero (literally, the Battle of the Shoemaker), named for a gap in the hills where

Mazamitla plaza

a group of insurgents fought their Royalist adversaries in 1812.

Mazamitla saw further military action during the ill-fated French Intervention in the middle of the nineteenth century but lost all its early archives which were burnt during the fighting.

Many of the old buildings around the central plaza of Mazamitla still preserve their colonial charm. The plaza has an arcade along one side, and the beautiful wooden balconies so characteristic of Jaliscan mountain towns are much in evidence. The church was rebuilt in 1957, on the site of an old adobe (mud-brick) building. It is always worth stepping inside to admire the magnificent floral arrangements adorning the simple interior. Its unusual exterior is, appropriately for the mountains, positively Norwegian in style.

Tasty, home-cooked Mexican food is served in the inexpensive restaurant behind the well-stocked corner store on the northern side of the plaza, opposite the church. The walls of the patio are decorated with old photographs of Mazamitla, and birds in cages sing for their supper. Alternatively, try eating in my personal favourite, La Troje, opposite the gasoline station. The cuisine here is what might be termed nouveau-Mexican. Their *trifajitas* is a truly sizzling sensation.

While today the town has several highly recommendable eating houses, forty years ago the situation was very different and positively do-it-yourself. Then, A. t'Serstevens wrote, "Mazamitla reminded me of the villages of Old Castille: white houses, pink at the base, very projecting roofs. We dined in a miserable posada, but my wife took over the kitchen stove and, amid an admiring but mute crowd of onlookers, prepared an admirable repast."

These days, there is no need to prepare your own food unless you particularly want to. Even so, many visitors bring a picnic lunch and choose one or another of an almost bewildering range of good spots in the surrounding woods in which to spread their tablecloth and lay out their silver. No need to bring your own venison or even hunting gear, since, according to etymologists, "Mazamitla" derives from an expression which means "place of arrows for hunting deer."

On the edge of the forest south of town, the tourist centre of Monteverde has well-built, comfortable wooden cabins which are ideal for family groups. Monteverde lacks a restaurant but the cabins all have stoves. Tucked away inside the nearby sprawling residential development of Los Cazos (The Cooking Pots) is El Salto, a 30 metre waterfall in the pine forest. On your way in, you will pass the Enchanted Garden, missed by many first-time visitors, where a series of waterfalls and streams tumble down gentle slopes through well-planned gardens. There is something Japanese about the Enchanted Garden with its rock pools and quaint wooden bridges, heightening the cosmopolitan flavour of the town.

And, before you leave Mazamitla, as long as you're not driving, why not try its culinary claim-to-fame, a drink called *pajarete,* a powerful combination of milk, *aguardiente* (firewater), brown sugar and chocolate?

Typical street in Mazamitla

If you can time your visit to coincide with a local fiesta, then try for early December when, from the 4th until the 12th, Mazamitla celebrates the fiesta of Guadalupe, February 24th, Flag Day or the last week in July, the party in honour of Saint Christopher.

And if you find a pretty *señorita* and want to ask for her hand in marriage? Then take care, for there is still a strong local custom which prevents you from running off with her without first asking permission from her father, giving him cigarettes and a bottle of spirits. Should he refuse, you are allowed to run off together – but by way of later repentence you will be expected to appear at the altar with your loved one dressed in black and carrying a cross.

The road between the town and Lake Chapala offers outstanding views of the lake, and of the scarp face which defines its southern edge. On a clear day it is easy to pick out Ajijic and Chapala on the far side, and Scorpion and Mezcala islands in the middle of the lake. During wildflower season (September and October) the meadows either side of the road become a blaze of colour, making the drive still more enjoyable. The road goes through the small town of La Manzanilla de la Paz, named for its abundance of *tejocotes,* the fruit, something like a crab-apple, of the Mexican hawthorn, *Crataegus mexicana,* and for its reputation as a peace-loving place. The farming vocabulary used by the town's residents still betrays their ancient Tarascan roots; for example, instead of *morral,* the usual Jaliscan word for a small bag, they say *chitara.*

Slightly further from the main road is Concepción de Buenos Aires. This town, though it looks like an old settlement, is in fact very young, having been founded in 1869. The road to Concepción de Buenos Aires passes very close to the ex-hacienda of Toluquilla which has a fine, 300-year-old aqueduct. From Chapala or Guadalajara, it takes about two hours to drive to Mazamitla.

Tamazula and its Scenic Valley

Those preferring an alternative return route or a lower-altitude, and consequently warmer, overnight stop, should consider visiting the town of Tamazula. It is about an hour's drive, and a very pretty one, along Highway 110 from the pine forests surrounding Mazamitla down to the broad valley where Tamazula lies. On the way you pass the buildings (now largely ruins) of the former hacienda of Contla.

Tamazula, "place of frogs", was settled from pre-Columbian times and known to the Spanish from as early as 1522, though it wasn't formally conquered until two years later. Silver was discovered here in 1567 and the town became a rich silver-mining and hacienda centre through the seventeenth and eighteenth centuries, declining after 1796 as the ores were worked out.

The Guzmán brothers, Francisco and Gordiano, who were both key independence fighters, were born here, and the town's full name is "Tamazula de Gordiano" in honour of the younger brother who survived the independence war and later resumed arms to fight the Americans in 1847.

In early years, the town saw its fair share of natural disasters, including a devastating earthquake in 1568 and a fall of ash from Colima volcano in 1606. In the eighteenth century it endured extremes of temperature and rainfall and survived even when the river Tamazula, which forms a natural southern boundary to the town, changed its course.

Its main church houses a sculpture of Our Sacred Lady, dating from 1563 and credited with having stopped the spread of cholera in the epidemic of 1850, not only in Tamazula but also in outlying parishes where it was taken in procession. A copy of this sculpture still makes annual rounds of the churches in the area. The temple of the Virgin of Guadalupe is also considered a fine colonial monument.

The area's major hacienda at the end of the sixteenth century was owned by a clergyman and produced, on irrigated land, wheat and vegetables, apples, pomegranates, oranges, olives, watercress, mint and ginger. The production of olives was something of a rarity in colonial Mexico, since the motherland didn't want competition for her own olive producers. Almost certainly the production in Tamazula was strictly for clerical consumption.

A sugar factory was opened, after the Revolution, in 1923. It was one of the first to have no cropland of its own, a major innovation at the time. The factory provided a service for the many farmers and landowners in the broad Tamazula valley.

Its founders chose Tamazula since it was a large town, with a strategic position in an irrigated valley with good communications, where cane had been grown for centuries, and because it wasn't part of an existing hacienda or in an area of radical agrarian activists. They were able to buy all the necessary machinery cheaply, and bring in labour, from factories which had problems of their own.

Their first milling was in 1924 and the factory quickly grew in importance, always paying a premium price, thereby guaranteeing a sufficient supply of cane. Its capital was greatly increased after 1959 in response to the much greater international demand for Mexican sugar following the Cuban Revolution.

The factory remains the pillar of the local economy though, on several occasions in recent years, state authorities have ordered its temporary closure for being in breach of anti-pollution regulations.

Persuasive travellers can sometimes talk their way into an accompanied tour of the plant, an interesting, if somewhat noisy, experience. It will change your perception of just what's involved in producing that spoonful of sugar you add to your coffee.

And the best place to stay? Just north of the town is the Hotel Real de la Loma, which has clean, comfortable spacious rooms and a huge swimming pool. Best of all, the water in the pool, and for the two-person tubs in the rooms, is thermal, coming from a hot-water spring at the base of the hill. The hotel overlooks the lovely Tamazula river and its valley, a valley which is green with sugar-cane year-round, a refreshing change in the dry season from the normally brown and withered Mexican countryside.

Perhaps the best time to visit is during the town's main fiesta, which begins in mid-January and ends on February 2nd. But, if you plan to stay overnight during this time, be sure to book early – the town gets very full.

• • •

15. The City of Colima and Its Surrounding Countryside

T he main highway between Guadalajara and Manzanillo, used by thousands of travellers a day, completely bypasses the medium-sized city of Colima. The city, where the four-lane, high speed tollroad narrows to a single lane each way, is seen only as an impediment to the rapid transit of traffic. Thus, travellers never have the chance to appreciate the considerable charm of this provincial state capital.

Not surprisingly, given its administrative functions, the city has a full range of tourist services with hotels and restaurants of every category. The tourist office, at Portal Hidalgo 20, is always helpful in providing information about the city's major tourist attractions which include museums, old buildings and several parks.

Colima has a particularly fine archaeological museum, the Museum of Western Cultures "María Ahumada", in the Casa de la Cultura complex, where many superb examples of pre-Hispanic Colima animal figurines can be seen. The city has another interesting museum, dedicated to the Dance, Masks and Popular Art of the West, located at Manuel Gallardo and 27 de Septiembre, in the University Fine Arts Institute. One of the largest collections of antique cars in Latin America, privately assembled over many years by Captain Francisco Zaragoza, is also in the city. It contains more than 350 vehicles, the oldest dating from 1884, but, sadly, is no longer open to the public.

In the Parque San Francisco de Almoloyan stand the ruins of a Franciscan monastery, begun in 1554 when the city had only 38 married citizens. Another of the city parks is known as the Parque de la Piedra Lisa (Smooth Stone Park), after the peculiarly-shaped rock which outcrops there. Local lore, perhaps aided and abetted by tourist promoters, claims that anyone who slides down this rock will one day return to the city.

The downtown area of the city, given a facelift a few years ago, is a pleasure

Volcán de Fuego from San Antonio

to walk around, especially compared with so many larger and much noisier Mexican state capitals. None of the buildings is especially old, however. The Hidalgo Theatre was built in the late nineteenth century on a property originally donated to the city by Father Miguel Hidalgo, of independence fame, when he was priest of Colima in 1792. The neoclassic sandstone cathedral on one side of the plaza dates from the same period, as does the State Government Palace, which in its interior has murals depicting Mexican history, painted by local artist, Jorge Chávez. On the south side of the plaza is a beautifully remodelled former hotel, now the Colima History Museum. The building was owned for many years by the De la Madrid family whose son, Miguel, was national President in the 1980's. The plaza's tall, elegant palm trees shade an ornate bandstand where local brass bands give free concerts most Wednesdays and Sundays. The nineteenth century *portales,* well-kept gardens, and streets designed for use by pedestrians as much as by vehicles, make city life as lived in Colima seem positively appealing.

Views of The Volcan De Fuego.

Few visitors to Colima realise how attractive the scenery of the northern part of the state is. What's more, good paved roads in the area make for easy access from the state capital.

Even half a day is sufficient to enjoy the first suggested drive, which offers unrivalled views of the active volcano called the Volcán de Fuego, or Volcán Colima, from which the state derives its name. The word "Colima" means "god of fire who dominates", but, despite its name, most of the volcano is in fact in the neighbouring state of Jalisco, and not Colima. Our route begins from Quesería, 27 kilometres northeast of Colima, on both the old road and the new *autopista* towards Ciudad Guzmán and Guadalajara. From Quesería a winding road skirts the lower slopes of the volcano.

Past some sugarcane fields, green even in the middle of the dry season, a small lake and the red roofs of the cabins of Carrizalillo park come into view on the left. The park is so poorly signposted it is easy to miss. This is one of several picnicking spots along the route where cold beers and soft drinks are normally available. Carrizalillo park is not as well maintained as it deserves, but it is hard to imagine a more idyllic spot from which to admire the impressively steep and barren upper slopes of the Volcán de Fuego. Sitting on the grass beside the placid waters of the lake... this is definitely a place to linger awhile.

The main road eventually ends at a T-junction. To the right (northwards) drive with caution because the bends are acute and parts of the road are unusually steep. This paved road ends at the ex-hacienda of San Antonio, once the hub of a massive coffee-growing operation, now being converted to a beautifully appointed hotel, complete with its own private chapel and extensive grounds. The graceful stone arches of a long aqueduct lend further charm to the hotel's driveway. Water spilling from the aqueduct helps to maintain the oasis of green that surrounds the buildings.

Ten minutes drive east of San Antonio, across a primitive rocky ford, is La María, a park with cabins of similar style to Carrizalillo but better maintained. While the Volcán de Fuego cannot be seen from here, La María's cabins offer simple accommodation for those who want to try the arduous climb to its summit, about nine kilometres away as the crow flies.

It should be pointed out here that the Volcán de Fuego, at (officially) 3960 metres or 12,992 feet high, is not as high as its sister volcano, the Nevado de

The Volcán de Fuego

I n the past 400 years, the Volcán de Fuego has been the most active volcano in Mexico, and indeed one of the most active in the world, having erupted at least 30 times since 1576. It is, not surprisingly, considered to be one of the country's most dangerous volcanoes.

On a geological time-scale, it began erupting about five million years ago in the Pliocene period, long after the nearby Nevado de Colima had ceased activity. It quickly developed into a large volcano which either partially blew apart or collapsed during Pleistocene times resulting in a caldera, five kilometres across. Since then a new cone developed inside the caldera. This new cone is the Volcán de Fuego as we see it today.

In historic times, the eruptions of the volcano have fallen into a definite cyclical pattern with periods of activity, each lasting about 50 years, interspersed with periods of dormancy. The first cycle of activity after the Spanish arrival in Mexico was between 1576 and 1611. Major eruptions ocurred in 1680 and 1690, and further complete cycles occurred between 1749 and 1818, and from 1869 to 1913. Most geologists agree that current activity is part of the fifth cycle, which began in 1961.

In each cycle, the first results of renewed activity force new lava into the existing crater. Once the crater has filled up, any additional lava is ejected from the crater and flows down the volcano's flanks. Later, the underground pressure which caused the activity is relieved, activity ceases, and the volcano enters another dormant phase. Even during this phase, a plume of hot gas often billows out from the volcano.

While the official height of the Volcán de Colima is always quoted as 3960 metres above sea level, during the late 1980's the true height was some 40 metres higher as a dome was pushed up inside the crater. The cone is built mainly of pyroclastic materials (ashes and volcanic bombs) of andesitic composition together with some basaltic lava, making it a classic example of a composite volcanic cone.

• • •

Colima, only eight kilometres further north, and also in Jalisco. The Nevado is Mexico's sixth highest peak; its summit is 4330 metres (14,206 feet) above sea level. Both the Nevado and the Volcán de Fuego are usually climbed from Atenquique to the east. The entire area around the two volcanoes was declared a National Park in 1936, though legislative snafus and bureaucratic apathy have prevented the implementation of effective conservation measures.

The main attraction of La María is the nearby lake which nestles in an enclosed wooded basin, the lower slopes of which have been planted with coffee bushes. This lake, teeming with carp, is a popular fishing and picnicking place.

Just off the most direct return route to Colima, via Comala, is Suchitlán, home of renowned mask-maker, Herminio Candelario Dolores, who also makes costumes for the region's folkloric dance troupes. Colourful examples of his masks hang in the museum of Dance, Masks and Popular Art referred to above.

Comala is a most attractive small town with whitewashed walls and red roofs, now considered to be a very desirable place of residence for people willing to commute the short distance into Colima to their office jobs. It has long been a favourite set for film-makers and has also figured prominently in Mexican literature. On the Colima side of the town, close to restaurants which cater mainly to a weekend crowd, is a co-operative venture which specialises in producing fine quality wooden furniture.

An Alternative Route to the Coast

My second recommended route, through very attractive rugged mountains and broad valleys, begins from the western outskirts of Colima city, goes through Minatitlán, and ends in the popular Pacific seaside resort of Manzanillo. While slightly longer in both distance and time than the toll highway between Colima and Manzanillo, this road provides a more scenic and cheaper alternative. There are no particular "must-sees" along this route; rather, it is a case of just ambling along, stopping for photographs and savouring the delightful scenery. Even if you have no intention of going all the way to Manzanillo, this is an enjoyable drive and an excellent way to see some of the countryside.

Minutes after leaving Colima the road crosses the River Armería on a bridge so wide and so high above the river that one wonders if its engineers made a miscalculation, a gross overestimate of the river's flow, before constructing it. But the innocent-looking stream that flows here most of the year belies the enormous power of the raging torrent that the Armería becomes after a storm. Just look at the size of some of the enormous boulders on the streambed if you don't believe me! Perched in anticipation on the wires alongside the road, belted kingfishers, flycatchers and American kestrels watch and wait for their next meal. Overhead, turkey vultures circle lazily on a thermal looking for carrion and roadkills.

The large hill to the northwest is the Cerro Grande, a limestone karst area, riddled by some of the largest cave systems in Mexico, including a 241-metre vertical shaft, the eighth biggest in the Americas, called El Pozo Blanco. According to legend, the nearby stone of Juluapan guards the entrance to the pre-Hispanic tomb and treasure of a former King of Colimán (now Colima), Ix. The treasure is reputed to include jewels brought from the Far East by Ix's Chinese friend, Wang

Colima Dogs, Past and Present

In many shaft tombs, superb, highly artistic, clay figures of dogs have been found. The clay figures, known as *izcuintlis* by collectors, have a highly polished rich warm red colour. They represent the deity Xolotl, in his role as guider of souls in the underworld and also provide some symbolic food for the departed on his or her journey. Dogs played an important part in the diet of Indian tribes in much of Mexico, and the *izcuintlis* invariably have appropriately corpulent bodies. They are believed to be modelled on the hairless dogs of the *Xoloitzcuintli* (pronounced Sholloitz-quintli) breed, common in pre-Columbian times, and now recognised as the oldest indigenous American domesticated dog. Its nearest relative is the Crested Dog of Manchuria; long ago, the two breeds must have shared a common ancestor.

Xoloitzcuintlis were in imminent danger of extinction in the 1940's, but an energetic campaign by the Mexican Kennel Club succeeded in reestablishing the breed as a domestic pet, this time not for eating but for sound medical reasons. Parents of asthmatic children discovered that the dogs, since they are hairless and consequently flealess, made ideal pets for their offspring. Research in those parts of Mexico where the breed still existed showed that villagers often slept with their dogs at night, as prevention against or cure for such ailments as malaria, rheumatism and the common cold. The dogs have body temperatures several degrees hotter than most breeds and snuggling up to one in bed is like having a hot water bottle beside you.

And, apart from having no hair, what do *Xoloitzcuintli* look like? They are normally slim with graceful, uniform grey or brown bodies, somewhat like a large Manchester Terrier. They have erect ears, similar to dogs portrayed in pre-Columbian frescoes at Tula and Cholula, stand about half a metre tall at the shoulder, and weigh up to 16 kilos.

This account is based on the chatty and informative writings of Norman Wright, former British Military Attache in Mexico, who was one of the prime movers of the Kennel Club campaign.

• • •

Wei, who crossed the Pacific regularly to visit him.

The road, in its path around the Cerro Grande, tries hard to follow the contours along the valleyside of the Juluapan river, a tributary to the Armería, but time and again has to descend to cross one of the Juluapan's own tributaries. These small streams, unlike most others in this part of the world, have water in them virtually all year. They add a dash of variety to the landscape. Their fast-flowing water dances over moss-covered rocks and they sing as they race down the valley. On their banks, huge white butterflies, attracted by a profusion of colourful wildflowers, flutter about in the foliage. An iguana, disturbed while sunning itself on exposed rocks, dashes for cover. If only you'd remembered to bring your gold pan....

It takes an hour to reach Minatitlán, which is the midway point. Close to the town is the Peña Colorada mine, a gigantic open-cast pit from which vast quantities of iron-ore for Mexico's steel industry have been extracted. The road towards Manzanillo goes straight through the neat, planned settlement which was built for mine workers.

The second part of the route, passing through a succession of tiny three or four house hamlets, turns and twists as it searches for a way through the hills that mask any view of the Pacific. Suddenly, with no advance warning, it emerges in the very heart of Manzanillo, only minutes from the resort's hotel strip.

Tampumacchay – Ancient Tombs, Modern Amenities

Ten minutes south of Colima city, along the toll highway to Manzanillo, is the turn to the east for Tampumacchay (sometimes spelt Tampu Machay), a family owned hotel-restaurant-archaeological centre.

It has been known for years that the area has enormous archaeological significance, and ceramic items of the Los Ortices culture, named for the nearest small village, are well represented in national museums and private collections. An excellent private collection, with all the right permits, is on display at the entrance to the hotel. It includes many fine and unusual pieces.

But even the original owners were surprised when, only months after opening their hotel, a series of shaft tombs were discovered on the property. Several of these tombs are now open to the public and add considerable interest to a visit to Tampumacchay. The hotel charges a small "tuition fee" for a guided visit to see the tombs which date from about 200 AD.

In Mexico, shaft tombs exist only in the western part of the country (Jalisco, Colima, Nayarit and Michoacán), and nowhere else. Similar tombs have, however, been found in Panama, Ecuador and Colombia, far to the south. That the shaft tombs' nearest neighbours are in Central and South America begs the question as to the possibility of oceanic Pacific coast contacts between Mexico and elsewhere in pre-Columbian times. While no direct evidence proving such contacts has ever been found, it does seem likely that there were some connections. For example, maize and *frijoles* (kidney beans) both native to Mexico, seem to have spread rapidly to South America, whilst peanuts and potatoes probably came in the opposite direction. These diffusions may have occurred as a result of human contacts between the two areas. Furthermore, some Nahuatl and Maya words appear, with identical forms and meanings, in some South American languages which scholars see as further evidence of probable trading connections.

Returning to Tampumacchay, its setting is surprising. As one approaches the entrance, the landscape seems monotonously flat and uninspiring, but the hotel is built on the edge of a very prominent ravine, with dramatic views across to the far side.

The area is typical semi-arid scrubland with a mixture of trees, small bushes, cacti and agaves. The permanent watercourse in the bottom of the ravine provides ideal conditions for a variety of wildlife and birds. Bambi, a tame white-tailed deer, grazes peacefully below the restaurant. Ground squirrels run, jump and burrow on the side of the valley. A short distance away, the endemic white-throated magpie-jay, a magnificent bluish jay with an extremely long tail, is both audible and visible, along with brightly-coloured, yellow-bellied tropical kingbirds.

Besides tours to the shaft tombs, the hotel also organizes half-day adventures into an extensive cave-system, a bumpy twenty minute drive away. The route underground traverses a hillside, with its entrance and exit at different points – there's no turning back once you embark on this one.

The system's large caverns have some well-developed formations, mainly stalactites, and areas of sparkling diamond-like gypsum crystals. This is no trip for the elderly or infirm since it involves crawling along on your belly at various points, and there is no illumination apart from the guides' helmet-lanterns, and whatever flashlights you may have thought to bring along.

After clambering through dusty caverns, you'll welcome a refreshing dip in the large, sparklingly-clear swimming pool. The gardens are just as immaculately kept and, in addition, decorated with pre-Columbian figures, some original, some copies of items found locally. The garden setting of these sculptures allows one to examine them from all sides and speculate on the imagination, ingenuity and craftsmanship of the people who made them. Visiting the shaft tombs causes one to speculate still further on the symbolism of burying important personages deep underground in specially-prepared chambers, and on the rituals which must have been observed on such occasions.

The hotel is still in its infancy with only a few rooms available for overnight guests but the restaurant is in full swing – almost literally, since it is reached by crossing a wood-and-rope walkway-bridge suspended over the garden. The menu is unpretentious, the cooking good. Because the restaurant doubles as a local night-spot, there is often live music. This is sometimes unnecessarily loud, given that the nearest competing noise comes from the cattle about five miles away.

For an environmental/cultural get-away-from-it-all weekend, try Tampumacchay, easy to enjoy, if difficult to pronounce.

• • •

Shaft Tombs

S haft tombs are underground burial chambers dating from pre-Columbian times. Most were dug between about 300 B.C .and 600 A.D. though their origins stretch back at least as far as 1500 B.C.

They have proved to be a rich source of archaeological data, although most have been looted before being examined by professional archaeologists. There are probably thousands of them but they are usually found by accident since normally little, if any, evidence of their presence exists on the surface.

The bones of individuals buried in shaft tombs show that many were taller (1.71 metres) than most pre-Hispanics, with deliberately deformed heads and other bone mutilations. Burial offerings included musical instruments and other objects made of ceramics, shells, stones and obsidian.

Some have interconnecting chambers constructed at different depths. This may indicate a hierarchy of burials in which the deeper ones, in more elaborately decorated chambers with richer offerings, are the high class section of the tomb.

Multiple burials in a single tomb are common. Some appear to include the sacrifice of other members of the same family, or of family servants. Sometimes the bodies were arranged so that all the heads face a certain direction – there are also examples where men were buried in one direction, and women in the opposite direction.

Many shaft tombs must have been built in advance of the death of the person buried there. They would have taken weeks to construct with the stone tools at the people's disposal and, in some cases, the entrance passages are too narrow for the body to have been manoeuvered along them after rigor mortis.

Ceramic pieces found in shaft tombs have included numerous examples of Colima animal art, beautifully proportioned dogs, armadillos and other animals, and of Ixtlán del Rio caricatures (page 119), reminiscent of modern cartoon-characters.

The most revealing ceramic finds portray entire Nayarit village scenes in which numerous figures, shown participating in some ceremonial occasion, or seated outside their houses, are mounted on a common base. These village scenes are unique to Western Mexico – no other Mexican pre-Columbian culture developed anything even vaguely similar – and are rich sources of information about everyday life.

• • •

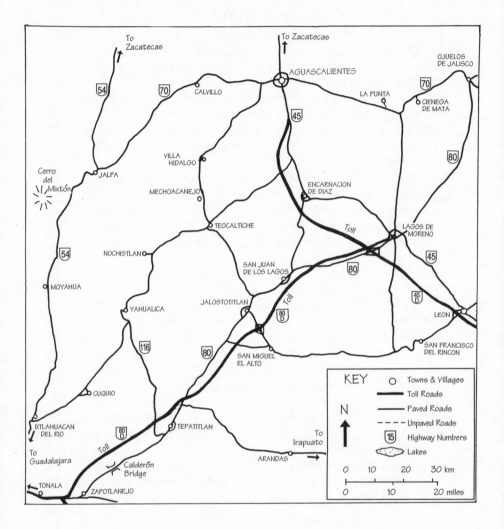

Part Four

16. From Guadalajara to San Juan de los Lagos

Northeast of Guadalajara is a region completely different from other parts of western Mexico: the high plains of Los Altos. This is a rich agricultural and ranching area and the early settlers recognised its potential soon after they colonised New Spain. Many of the haciendas were lavishly decorated and have survived largely intact to the present day.

Los Altos was a wild, border zone and the settlers had to ward off repeated attacks by marauding bands of Chichimeca Indians who refused to bow to the Spanish crown. The region proved to have mineral riches, too, and the larger towns founded by the Spanish became important trading centres for supplies and for metal ores, especially silver. They had to be fortified to protect shipments of the precious metal from bandits. In some places, the fortifications still remain.

Religion also played a decisive role. Miraculous occurrences in San Juan de los Lagos gave rise to an enormous following for the Virgin of Candlemas. In nearby Lagos de Moreno, many religious orders constructed places of worship, meditation and instruction. In the 1920's, as politicians strove to outlaw the church, so church militants determined to destroy the social fabric, in the armed Cristeros rebellion.

The route suggested here can easily be extended to include one or more of three outstanding colonial cities: Zacatecas, Guanajuato and San Miguel de Allende. These cities have art, architecture, museums, hotels and restaurants worthy of an entire book to themselves and each of these cities is well described in any good tourist guide.

Towns en Route

The Los Altos area has such an excellent network of main roads that a good road map will prove more useful than a written description of how to combine the many interesting towns into a logical route.

Highway 80 which goes north-eastwards from Guadalajara into the Los Altos region provides access to several captivating places. Tepatitlán is a bustling, commercial town bypassed by main roads. Its centre preserves a Victorian charm with a flowery, wrought-iron bandstand and plenty of trees. It has a definite air of affluence.

A short distance north of Tepa – most of the Los Altos towns are affectionately known by less than half their real name – is a road for Manuel Doblado and Irapuato. This route, which provides a scenic alternative for travellers to Querétaro and Mexico City, passes through Arandas. The church of San José in Arandas is

The Upside-Down Map

The toll highway from Guadalajara to San Juan de los Lagos may be faster but the old main road passes the site of one of the first major battles in the Mexican War of Independence.

On the morning of Thursday, 17th of January, 1811, eighty thousand ill-equipped rebel supporters of Father Miguel Hidalgo, led by Ignacio Allende, faced a smaller, but more professional, Royalist army fighting to smash the Independence movement. A stray grenade which landed right in the middle of the insurgents' ammunition supplies brought a premature end to the fighting and Allende, Hidalgo and their men fled the scene in complete disarray. Losing this battle prolonged the eleven-year war and Mexico had to wait until 1821 to receive her independence.

The battle took place by Calderón bridge, and a statue of Hidalgo, arms aloft, marks the general area. The historical curiosity is that the commonly accepted plan of the battleground, as depicted in hundreds of textbooks and museums around the country, has its north arrow pointing directly south. There are many topsy-turvy aspects to the Battle of Calderón but perhaps this is the strangest of all. Detailed study of air photos and the site by Bárcenas (1986) proved the correct orientation beyond all doubt.

There are four bridges in the vicinity. The one where the battle was fought has a commemorative plaque on it, erected on the centenary of the battle. It was made a National Monument in 1932. No one is sure what the vegetation was like in this area at the time of the battle, but today be prepared to encounter spiky acacia bushes, mesquite plants and only limited shade. The shade that does exist is mostly provided by the distinctive white-flowering morning-glory tree.

• • •

one of the finest neogothic churches in western Mexico. Outside its main entrance sits the biggest bell ever cast anywhere in the country, some say the third biggest in the world, so big that it was never hung and never rung, its weight being considered too dangerous for the structure. May it rest in peace!

The main highway from Tepatitlán continues towards San Juan de los Lagos passing through Jalostotitlán, from where another highway cuts off east to León via San Miguel el Alto. Jalostotitlán has an attractive central plaza. Nearby, beneath the Tamara hill, locals claim an entire city is buried underground. Don't explore too much, for the villagers also say that it is protected by a seven-headed rattle-snake, which appears every year on Good Friday.

San Miguel el Alto has the only plaza in Mexico with pink sandstone arcades on all four sides. All its important buildings, including the town hall and parish church, are constructed of the same rock, giving the town a harmony rarely found elsewhere.

Between Jalostotitlán and San Juan de los Lagos is the junction for the Teocaltiche road which eventually goes to Aguascalientes. The centre of Teocaltiche also has colonial charm with several old buildings including the lovely former hospital, now Teocaltiche's *Casa de la Cultura* (House of Culture). Outside the town, an archaeological zone, called Cerro Encantado, has mounds and various underground chambers. Fifteen kilometres north of Teocaltiche in Mechoacanejo is a very interesting un-named museum with archaeological pieces, firearms (which include one of John Wayne's guns), and coins. The priest who started this museum wanted to prove to his parishoners that everything has its value – all the items displayed here were, at one time or another, considered worthless junk!

San Juan de los Lagos

A town of narrow streets, San Juan de los Lagos is a place visited by several million Mexicans each year on account of its religious significance, but by a surprisingly small number of foreigners.

There are several different versions as to what happened in 1623, when the Virgin of Candlemas performed her most famous miracle. Some say a ten-year-old child, the daughter of a circus acrobat, died when she was accidentally impaled on a dagger, to the immense distress of her loving family. The child's nurse put a figurine of the Virgin on the body. Others relate that it was the acrobat himself who fell and became impaled on a dagger. His wife placed the Virgin on his body and prayed. Whichever version is more accurate, to the amazement of all, the dead person regained consciousness, fully recovered, with no sign of any wound. The Virgin was offered to the church but it was considered appropriate that it first be professionally restored. To this end, it was carefully wrapped and then sent to Guadalajara. When it was unwrapped for examination by the experts, it was found that somehow, somewhere along the way, it had already been magically and completely restored.

Souvenirs for religious pilgrims

On its return, the statue was first stored in the church vestry for eight years, then put in its rightful place of honour in San Juan's main church. It has continued to assist people in need ever since. The faithful will walk or shuffle on their knees for days to pay adequate homage to this marvellous little statue which is made of toasted *agave quiote*   or cornstalk dough. The church was later raised in status to a Basilica.

San Juan holds a huge fair to honour the Virgin, beginning January 20th each year and ending on the 2nd of February, Candlemas day. This mammoth fiesta, one of the oldest in Mexico, has dances, among them the famous one in which the Christians take on the Moors, fireworks, cock-fights, horse races and gala balls. It is a time of pilgrimage for people from all over the country. The crowd that assembles is one of the largest annual gatherings in Mexico, surpassed only by the multitudes who attend the celebrations in Mexico City at the Shrine of Guadalupe, the country's patron saint, on December 12th.

Whatever time of the year you visit San Juan you will be amazed at the number of street stalls selling religious artifacts including *milagros,*   the silver charms in the shapes of limbs, hearts, heads and animals, which the faithful will offer to their favourite saint in the hope of receiving a favour.

The Holy War, 1926-1929.

B oth the Reform Laws of 1857 and the 1917 Constitution, ratified even before the end of the Mexican Revolution, sought to restrict the rights and privileges of the Church, divorcing it completely from the State. Plutarco Elías Calles who was President of Mexico between 1924 and 1928 went several steps further and in mid-term banned priests from teaching in primary schools, speaking against the Constitution or wearing clerical garments in public. Some of the Catholic priests in Jalisco and neighbouring states began armed opposition to Calles who responded with brutal force. Many priests were summarily executed while others fled their rural parishes for the relative safety of larger towns and cities. The armed religious uprising became known as the Cristeros War since one of the battle cries of the Catholic fighters was "*¡Viva Cristo Rey!*" (Long live Christ the King!) Sixteen Jaliscan heroes of this armed struggle, which has never been officially condoned by the Catholic church, were beatified in 1992. Beatification is the first step on the road to sainthood.

The anti-clerical articles of the 1917 Constitution were revoked by President Salinas de Gortari's government in 1992 when full diplomatic relations with the Vatican were resumed.

• • •

The Virgin Who Plays Marbles...

The Virgin of San Juan de los Lagos sometimes comes to life and plays marbles. She makes the marbles herself using mud. The place from where she takes the mud is called the *"pocito de la Virgen"*, the little well of the Virgin. During fiesta time, devotees visit this little well and rub mud over themselves to ease away their aches and pains. Some enterprising local merchants even sell small mud cakes which have an image of the Virgin stamped on them.

• • •

If a favour is granted, the same faithful will then commission a *retablo,* traditionally a small painting on tin, folk-art rather than fine art, which will also be given to the church. Many churches in Mexico house fine collections of these thanks-givings and the San Juan Basilica is no exception. Many portray car accidents and train wrecks from which people have had narrow escapes; others depict hospital wards where a close relative was interned at death's door but restored to full health. The problems that Mexicans wishing to migrate to the U.S. sometimes experience are also alluded to in retablos; my favourite is one with a colour photocopy of a successful applicant's Green Card.

As one might expect, the Basilica, built between 1732 and 1769, is a sumptuous building, predominantly neoclassic in style, with a fine altar (originally intended for a church in Rome) and numerous excellent paintings, including six canvases signed by Rubens. There are many other fine old colonial buildings in the town and it is worth calling in at the Tourist Office, near the Basilica, for a detailed street plan showing their exact locations.

The town has another large fair each year during the first twelve days of December.

The entire Los Altos area is renowned for high-quality sewing and San Juan is no exception. Here is a good place to seek out artistic designs in cross-stitch, drawn-thread work and embroidery. The shops in San Juan also stock a wide selection of dresses, blouses, tablecloths and woollen items such as *sarapes* . Another speciality of this region is candy. The variety of shapes, colours and flavours on display is a delight, not only to the eye, but also to all sweet-tooths.

• • •

17. Lagos de Moreno
The Athens of Jalisco

L agos de Moreno is a town with a charming ambience. A succession of small squares with old trees and gardens, connected by shaded streets, gives it a cultured university air. At every turn there are beautifully kept old buildings to be enjoyed and it is absolutely fitting that the town, in its entirety, should have been declared a national monument.

Boasting more than 380 cultural and historic sites (or sights) the town is known, with good reason, as the Athens of Jalisco. Its peak coincided with the governments of President Porfirio Díaz in the late 1800's when local haciendas produced both an aristocratic elite and plenty of money enabling them to enjoy what they considered were the better things in life.

There are better hotels here than elsewhere in Los Altos. An overnight stay allows visitors to savour the unique atmosphere of this lovely town in the early morning or late evening when lower-angled sunlight shows the colours and details in the stonework to best effect.

Lagos was founded as Santa María de los Lagos in 1563 on the west bank of the broad Lagos river. It assumed its modern name in 1827. In early colonial times, its inhabitants had to withstand repeated attacks from the Chichimecas. When silver was discovered in large quantities near Zacatecas, further north, the town became a natural staging-post on the mule route to Mexico City, where all colonial silver was taken for assaying. At the same time, the main contraband route across Mexico, between Tampico, on the Atlantic, and San Blas, on the Pacific, passed through the town. As a result of this strategic location, the city was fortified with walls, some of which still remain. There are few examples in Mexico of colonial walled cities. Lagos is one of the best preserved.

The width of the river necessitated the construction of a bridge, at least for

La Rinconada Restaurant

more modern traffic, and in the eighteenth century Lagos Bridge was built on the northern edge of the town. This bridge is the subject of one of the charming tales in *El Alcalde de Lagos* (The Mayor of Lagos), a delightful collection of witty short stories compiled by Alfonso de Alba. The stories capture the provincial nature of the town perfectly, complete with the very different perceptions of the local intelligentsia and their rural *campesino* counterparts as the town grew to maturity.

The imposing ultrabaroque parish church of the Assumption is also eighteenth century and looks onto the principal plaza. Two blocks away, the former Capuchinas convent has been converted into the *Casa de la Cultura,* with a concert hall, spaces for art exhibits, library and music classes. Few *Casas de la Cultura* any-where in the country are housed in quite such an historic or magnificent building. Walk into the patio and see for yourself. The mural inside depicts Pedro Moreno, hero of the Independence movement, who was born near the town, and after whom the town is named. Another building in the Capuchinas square houses the Agustín Rivera Museum with its displays of archaeological and historical items.

Behind the parish church is the Rosas Moreno theatre, one of the few provin-cial theatres to have survived with its interior spaces and decorations unchanged from the end of the nineteenth century. This building, designed by Primitivo Serrano, was begun in 1887, and inaugurated in 1907. It is named in honour of locally born José Rosas Moreno, the Children's Poet.

Lagos de Moreno is home to a chain of antique shops, well worth visiting if only to admire the buildings themselves rather than the antiquities they contain. Near the centre of the town, on Hidalgo street, one store fills a classic colonial town-house. Five minutes out of town on Highway 80 towards San Juan de los Lagos, look for the Hacienda Montecristo where the showrooms occupy part of a beautifully restored country estate. The remainder of the hacienda is used as a private residence by the owner. The Montecristo antique shops are nationally famous and attract collectors from all over Mexico.

The central area of Lagos de Moreno, with its romantic corners and shaded walks, is a place to wander through slowly, savouring the sights and sounds of an unashamedly provincial town, one proud of its history and still retaining a dignified air.

Alternative Routes to Aguascalientes

From Lagos de Moreno there are two alternative routes to Aguascalientes. The first, much shorter, is via Encarnación de Díaz. Betwen Lagos and Encarnación, the ex-hacienda of El Mesón de los Sauces has murals painted on the walls of its corridors in a naïve style. Painted in 1881 by an unknown artist, they include the discovery of the Americas, the first mass held in the New World, and rare depictions of everyday family life of the time.

Encarnación de Díaz has a park with examples of topiary, and is also home to a museum about the Cristeros religious fighters.

The alternative route from Lagos to Aguascalientes goes further north to the continental divide at Ojuelos de Jalisco, a town on the state border with Zacatecas. Ojuelos was built as a fortress settlement to protect caravans of silver being transported in colonial times from the northern mines in Zacatecas and San Luis Potosi to Mexico City. The fortress, *El Fuerte,* which dates from 1568, has been restored and, complete with towers and battlements, is now the town hall. There are many other old buildings in Ojuelos including the neoclassic San José church and a former stage-coach post.

Thirty-three kilometres from Ojuelos, this northern route passes the hacienda of Ciénega de Mata, belonging to the Rincón Gallardo family. Many members of this family played distinguished roles in Mexican history in both military and civil matters. Their hacienda, founded in the sixteenth century, quickly became one of the largest and most important of the region. It is still in a beautiful state of repair with a particularly magnificent chapel. The main house has a mural by Icaza showing the sport of *charrería* (horsemanship), for which the Rincón Gallardo family is famous. The hacienda is not normally open to the public but given its enormous importance in the history of the entire region, cannot be overlooked.

Even as early as 1700, it controlled an area of about 4500 square kilometres (1750 square miles) though only a small part was classed as arable land. Most of this area was in the present-day state of Aguascalientes and, indeed, the Aguascalientes Government Palace was originally the Rincón Gallardo townhouse. Ciénega de Mata constituted a veritable principality in its own right with an independent administration, its own cavalry, and a central village and castle, surrounded by a string of subordinate hamlets.

The vast social gulf that existed on the haciendas between their owners and their peon workers is perhaps nowhere better illustrated than at Ciénega de Mata. Here, if the landowner dropped anything, the peon never handed it back directly, but placed it first on the inverted brim of his own hat. The peon's wages were in coupons, redeemable for goods only in the hacienda store, together with a ration of salt and soap.

To the north of the highway, about fourteen kilometres nearer Aguascalientes, on the hacienda of La Punta, internationally famous fighting bulls have been raised since 1924. Also part of the Rincón Gallardo holdings, this ranch has hostel accommodation for anyone wishing to experience and take part in the day-to-day work of raising these ferocious beasts. Its buildings, mainly nineteenth century, include granaries, a bullring and the Great House.

• • •

18. Aguascalientes
The Charms of a Provincial City

F irst impressions of Aguascalientes as a modern, sprawling, thriving city
belie the colonial charm of its centre and the rich treasures to be found in
its many historic buildings. There are mysteries about Aguascalientes that no one
has yet solved. Why, for example, was a vast network of subterranean tunnels
constructed beneath the city? Today, these tunnels which gave rise to the city's
nickname, the Perforated City, are closed to visitors. Were they built originally as
part of some elaborate defensive plan by the early settlers in this wild, frontier
region? Whole armies hid in them during the turbulent times of the Revolution.

Aguascalientes city is the capital of the state of the same name. The area now
constituting the state of Aguascalientes, one of the smallest in Mexico, was, for
much of its history, part of the state of Zacatecas. The independence of Aguascalientes was sealed by a kiss, as the locals are invariably quick to point out. In
1835, General Antonio López de Santa Anna was engaged in putting down a
rebellion in Zacatecas. Between battles, he went partying and met María Luisa
Villa. He obviously found her very attractive since he asked for a kiss, promising
her anything she wanted in return. María Luisa, whose husband Pedro García
Rojas subsequently became the first Governor of Aguascalientes, seized her
opportunity, and in response to a passionate kiss, requested autonomy for her
native region. If Santa Anna hadn't been a man of his word, there wouldn't have
been a pair of lips in the state's coat-of-arms.

The kiss, along with other memorable incidents in the area's history, is portrayed in the marvellous murals on the first floor of the Government Palace,
painted in 1961-62 by Oswaldo Barra, a Chilean disciple of Diego Rivera. The
murals have a vibrant intensity with vivid forms and colours. Here is the coming
of the railway to the city in 1884. Aguascalientes still has a superb station building

and some of the largest locomotive workshops in Latin America. The prosperity generated by the railways caused several fine hotels to be built at the turn of the century, including the Francia on the main square. The Francia's excellent gourmet restaurant has an interesting menu featuring many original dishes. How about delicately flavoured grape soup for example? The restaurant is worth seeing if only for the undeniable elegance of its decor.

Hotels have prospered in the city because, amongst other attractions, it boasts thermal spas. These, of course, gave rise to its name, which means Hot Waters. The spas are still a major attraction and the largest one, Ojocaliente, offers a variety of pools, saunas, steambaths and sports facilities. Another major attraction is the annual San Marcos fair. Shopping is good here, too. The discerning will find

Government Palace, Aguascalientes

bargains in colourfully-embroidered sarapes, blouses and dresses as well as in hand-crocheted and pottery items.

The Government Palace is well worth admiring, and not just for its murals. Parts of the building date from 1657, making it one of the oldest civil edifices in the city. It originally belonged to the Rincón Gallardo family, owners of Ciénega de Mata (page 112). Clearly no money was spared in its construction. The State Government bought it in 1856 and later added a second patio, choosing, with good judgement, to build it in a style identical to the original.

On a walk through the central area of the city, many visitors are surprised by the number of seventeenth and eighteenth century churches. Their façades differ greatly. The San Diego Church, built by the Barefoot Carmelites, was begun in 1682. The statues in its 1740 façade include representations of a French King and a Portuguese Queen. The city's cathedral, dating from 1704, may be big, but the quality of the stonework is nothing like as fine as that of the Temple of Guadalupe, begun in 1763. Near the cathedral is the very attractive Morelos Theatre, opened in 1885.

The San Antonio church, whose architect was self-taught local builder, Refugio Reyes, has curious towers and was built at the height of the city's boom between 1895 and 1908. European influence was strong during the *Porfiriato* (the 33-year period when Porfirio Díaz was in power) and this church has an organ from Germany, paintings from Italy, and ornaments from France. The bells, however, came from the United States.

Architecture aside, perhaps the most interesting church in Aguascalientes is the Encino church, located a discreet distance away from the central area on its own small plaza. Here, the image over the altar is of a black Christ, one of several black Christs in the country. The story is that, during the construction of the church, originally to be dedicated to Saint Michael the Archangel, a vision appeared in the trunk of a nearby *encino* or oak tree, of Christ on the Cross. The black Christ is an exact replica of what was seen.

Next to the Encino Church is a small but important museum, featuring the work of José Guadalupe Posada (1852-1913), an engraver whose work inspired such distinguished artists as José Clemente Orozco, Diego Rivera, and Alfredo Zalce. Posada's work has been much imitated but no one has successfully captured the spirit of his caricatured skeletons, *calaveras,* to the same effect. He produced more than twenty thousand beautifully crafted engravings and lithographs, many of them designed to educate and inform a large public who could neither read nor write. The son of an illiterate baker, Posada became recognised posthumously as the precursor of the Mexican art revolution, one of the first Mexican artists to produce truly Mexican designs.

Not surprisingly, Posada is included in the Government Palace mural. He is flanked by two other famous artists: Manuel M. Ponce, composer, who lived much of his youth in the city and Jesús Contreras, a one-armed sculptor born here.

Ponce (1882-1948) was to Mexican music what Posada was to Mexican art, composing hugely successful popular songs as well as using ideas derived from Mexican folkloric music in formal orchestral works. Many of his guitar compositions are now considered an essential part of the repertoire of any classical guitarist.

Contreras (1866-1902) studied in Europe at the time of Rodin. He was a prolific sculptor of public monuments and when plans were announced for monu-

The San Marcos Fair

T he San Marcos Fair, held from the second week in April to early May each year, attracts people from all over Mexico and many parts of the United States. It dates back to 1604 when a small indigenous Indian settlement, San Marcos, was founded within walking distance of the growing Spanish city of Aguascalientes. The fair's religious origins, long forgotten, have become Mexico's biggest State Fair, a lively, colourful three week spectacular, in which bullfights, folkloric dancing, mechanical games, cockfights, wine-tasting, cultural events and merrymaking all compete for visitors' attention.

Much of the activity associated with the fair takes place in the San Marcos Gardens, first laid out over a hundred years ago. Protected by pink stone balustrades and graceful wrought ironwork, thick foliage and tall trees shade romantic paths and fountains, providing a beautiful setting for this most exciting of fairs. The sounds of birdlife normally heard in the park are replaced by shouting and laughing, earnest conversations between young lovers, spectacular fireworks displays and the cries of innumerable ambulatory vendors selling everything from delicious chicken enchiladas and the local culinary speciality turkey in rich chocolate *mole* sauce, to candy floss, giant balloons, ingenious handcrafted toys and cheap souvenirs.

Stop and have your fortune told by a trained and supposedly clairvoyant canary, which selects your future from a deck of fortune cards; sample a meringue, engaging the vendor in the traditional, entertaining "Heads I pay, tails it's free" system of payment; watch the colourful folkloric dancing; listen to mariachis; see Mexico's top matadors in action at the San Marcos bullring; place your bets on fighting cocks in the modern Casino which houses Latin America's biggest *palenque*; or indulge in the time-honored tradition of watching or participating in the *paseo* in which young women walk around the park in one direction, young men in the other.

• • •

ments honouring two famous Mexicans from each of the Republic's States to be erected along Reforma, one of the principal avenues in Mexico City, Contreras was commissioned to do no fewer than nineteen of them.

Thirty minutes north of Aguascalientes is the Museum of the Insurgency, housed in the Hacienda San Blas in Pabellón de Hidalgo. This was the spot where Hidalgo, the rebel leader, was forced to relinquish command of his army, in favour of Ignacio Allende. Those interested in other side trips from Aguascalientes should consider driving to Tepezala or Arientos, both former mining towns, abandoned more than 200 years ago, and now neatly restored.

Driving in virtually any direction from Aguascalientes takes you into ranch and vineyard country. Grapes are considered such a major local product that the State even has them depicted in its coat-of-arms. Visitors interested in seeing first-hand the operations of local vineyards, or the cattle ranches where fighting bulls are raised, should ask their hotel for more information.

If you are looking for an alternative route back towards Guadalajara, and enjoy driving winding mountain roads, try taking Federal Highway 70 to Jalpa and then the very scenic Highway 54 to Guadalajara. This road, popularly called the *barrancas* (canyons) road, is not a very fast highway but the scenery is outstanding. Fifteen kilometres outside Guadalajara is a viewpoint and well-maintained small park named after the famous artist, Dr. Atl. The view from here encompasses not only the distant sierras and the confluence of two major valleys but also rocky escarpments and the splendid 120-metre-high Cola de Caballo Falls. This is one of Guadalajara's better kept secrets and one rarely visited by the casual tourist.

If you want to hike down into the canyon, the best place to start from is the small village of Huentitán el Alto on the northern edge of Guadalajara, beyond the planetarium and zoo. This arduous hike is only recommended for those in better-than-average physical condition.

• • •

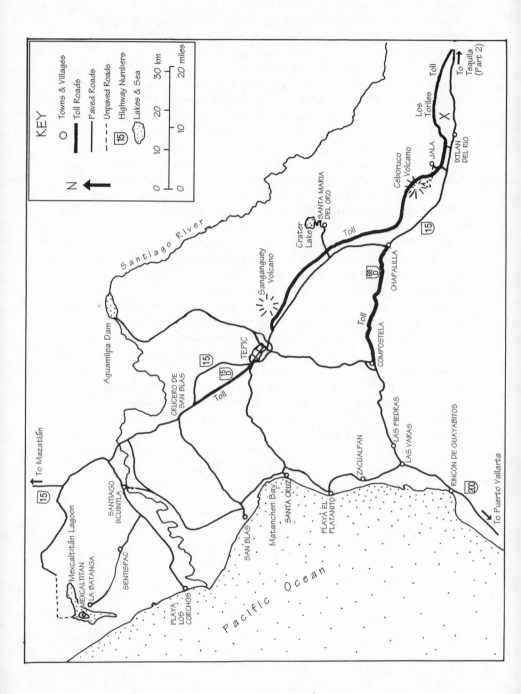

Part Five

19. The Route West to San Blas

T here are several worthwhile sidetrips on the drive from Guadalajara to the interesting old port of San Blas, once one of the most important ports on the Pacific coast. Leaving Guadalajara, Highway 15 first passes through Tequila and Magdalena (chapter 10) before crossing the Jalisco-Nayarit State line, where Central time gives way to Mountain time, and descending into Ixtlán del Río. The intriguing archaeological site of Los Toriles, very close to the town, is well worth a short visit. For those interested in longer side-trips, the drives up Ceboruco volcano or to Crater Lake provide totally different scenery to that of the remainder of the journey. The city of Tepic with its good hotels and restaurants is an ideal place to stay overnight if your sidetrips have used up the available daylight. The toll road alternative, Highway 15D is a much faster inter-city route.

Ixtlán del Río

The archaeological site of Los Toriles near Ixtlán del Río was probably inhabited from about the year 0. Only a few structures have been restored but these include a circular construction, one of only a handful of this shape ever found by archaeologists in Mexico. This round building, which probably served as the stage for dances and other celebrations, was dedicated to Quetzalcoatl, the Feathered Serpent, here in the guise of Ehecuatl, God of the Wind. The evidence for this is primarily in the cross-shaped apertures in the outer wall, inside which are the remains of an earlier structure. Obviously this part of the site was ceremonial in function.

On the hillside behind the restored buildings the residential areas included caves, and workshops for making obsidian arrow-heads and knives. Etymologists say that "Ixtlán" means "place of obsidian".

Many ceramic figures have been found in the area – so numerous and so distinctive that their style is known simply as Ixtlán. The artists responsible for these figures lived before 1300 A.D. Warriors wearing their armour, models of single dwellings with their inhabitants engaged in some domestic task, and grotesque, almost caricatured, human figures, usually seated and often with deformities, have all been found. The Regional Museums in Guadalajara, Colima and Tepic all have excellent collections of these figurines.

Mexico's Volcanic Axis

The Volcanic Axis is a broad belt of high relief which crosses Mexico from west to east. It contains virtually all the country's active and recently dormant volcanoes including Popocatepetl and Iztaccihuatl, Paricutín, (chapter 28) and Colima (chapter 15), still very active. It also includes the world's smallest volcano, only a few metres high, on the outskirts of the city of Puebla.

The shape of volcanoes was imitated by the Olmec people when they built their first pyramids. Today, legacies of previous volcanic activity are found in mud-volcanoes, geothermal activity, and the numerous hot-springs and spas scattered throughout the Volcanic Axis.

Geologists are not sure why the Axis exists. Most major tectonically active areas have been linked to the steeply dipping margins of tectonic plates, but Mexico's Volcanic Axis may be a rare example of activity associated with a gently dipping plate margin where the edge of the marine Cocos plate is subsumed at only a slight gradient beneath the North American plate.

Almost all the volcanic activity has taken place in the last 25 million years, from the upper Oligocene period, to the Recent. A study using Carbon-14 dating on the palaeosoils under twelve volcanoes near Toluca yielded ages ranging from 38,600 to 8,400 years; most of the literally hundreds of recognisable volcanic structures in Western Mexico are less than 50,000 years old.

Colima volcano is considered potentially dangerous since it is capped by a dacitic plug characteristic of a Pelean volcano. Such volcanoes have a nasty habit of erupting with the emission not of molten lava, but of less spectacular, but far more devastating, red-hot clouds of asphyxiating gases.

The western end of the Axis is broken up by the downfaulted troughs of Tepic, Chapala and Colima. These valleys have had marked effects on the drainage of the region, often resulting in enclosed lake basins. Some of these basins are now permanently, and others seasonally, dry.

• • •

There are several small hotels and restaurants in Ixtlán. The archaeological site is four kilometres east of the town. At the entrance to the town is the *Cerro de Cristo* (Hill of Christ) from which a fine panoramic view over the entire area may be enjoyed.

Ceboruco Volcano

A short distance further west on Highway 15 is Ceboruco volcano which has a cobblestone road to the top. The road starts from the old and picturesque village of Jala, eight kilometres off the main highway. The road up Ceboruco is a geologist's or biologist's dream come true, a slowly unfolding series of volcanic forms and different types of vegetation with abundant surprises even for the scientifically expert. Small wonder that the great German botanist, Karl Theodor Hartweg, was so impressed when he visited Ceboruco in the nineteenth century.

Near the top are several short but interesting walks, some in shady, thickly vegetated valleys hidden between towering walls of blocky lava, some along the many overlapping rims of the various old craters of which this complex peak is comprised. Wherever you choose to walk, a multicoloured profusion of flowers and butterflies will greet your eyes.

On the south side of an attractive grassy valley at kilometre sixteen, fumaroles send hot gases and steam high into the air in the volcano's final death throes before becoming irrevocably extinct. Ceboruco's first recorded eruption was in 1542 but the huge blocks of lava near the summit date from a prolonged series of eruptions in the 1870's.

Highway 15 cuts through Ceboruco's lava field a few kilometres after the Jala junction. For those not wishing to brave the cobblestone road up to the volcano, this is a good place to stretch the legs and marvel at the inhospitable, black lava blocks which were spewed out more than a hundred years ago.

La Laguna – Crater Lake

At kilometre 194, a short, perfectly paved road to the east first passes through the former mining town of Santa María del Oro and then, rising slightly, affords an absolutely splendid view of a beautiful slate-blue lake, La Laguna, set in the middle of a ring of verdant hills. This idyllic site, little developed at present, must surely become a major vacation spot in the future. For now it is an undiscovered oasis of beauty and tranquility and is, in reality, a drive-in volcanic crater. Around the lake are several small restaurants; the fish they serve jumps straight out of the lake and into the frying pan and is highly recommendable.

Bungalows and RV spaces are available for those who want to spend more time in this peaceful place, contemplating the serene waters of the lake and the outstanding natural beauty of the surrounding area. For reservations, write to Chris French, Apdo. 493, Tepic, Nayarit.

There are many attractive walks in the vicinity; a particularly pleasant and satisfying one is around the lake which has no encircling road, only a path. At an easy pace, this takes about an hour and a half and provides a wonderful range of lake and mountain views. Alternatively, a short climb to an abandoned gold mine offers a glimpse into the area's past and an opportunity to strike it rich. Or how about swimming or hiring a rowboat to venture out onto the lake?

Tepic

Tepic, the capital of the state of Nayarit, has the full range of tourist services as well as an outstanding regional museum, housed in the former headquarters of Barron, Forbes & Company, the nineteenth century customs agents of San Blas. The city is an excellent overnight stop even though most tourists will not find much to detain them for very long.

Near the centre of the city is the house where Amado Nervo, one of Mexico's most famous poets (1870–1919), was born. Indeed, Tepic is really a very Mexican city, where tourists are rarely encountered and where curio-selling street vendors are virtually unknown. It is worth looking at the historical murals in the Government Palace, the Temple of Santa Cruz with its grass cross, revered since the eighteenth century, and the nineteenth century cathedral with its slender towers.

Tepic is one of the closest cities to the remote and isolated mountainous areas still inhabited by the Huichol and Cora Indian tribes. Their very distinctive and much sought-after handicrafts of masks, beadwork and pictures made of coloured yarn artistically arranged on beeswax-coated boards to tell their tribal legends, are on sale in some of the city's shops.

From Tepic to San Blas there is a choice of routes: either continue along Highway 15 to the *Crucero* San Blas (San Blas crossroads) from where the road down to the port is clearly signposted or, alternatively, follow signs for Santa Cruz and Miramar. A few kilometres before entering Santa Cruz, a road for San Blas leaves towards the north. This road, with its series of spectacular coastal views, passes the area's best beach, Matanchen Bay.

• • •

20. San Blas
Historic Port on the Pacific

S an Blas, described in many guidebooks as some kind of undiscovered Poly-
nesian or Tahitian hideaway with thatched roofs and palm trees, was one
of New Spain's principal gateways for trade with the Far East in colonial times.

But later its position a short distance off the main coastal road north to
Mazatlán, (which eventually superceded San Blas as this region's main port), led
to a decline in its fortunes. This decline, together with the town's swamp-infested
hinterland with its abundance of midges and "no-see-ums", meant that San Blas
was slow to become a really popular tourist destination.

The first Europeans to explore San Blas, in May 1530, were led by Nuño
Beltrán de Guzmán, the Spanish conquistador and founder of Guadalajara. Guzmán was intent on exploring as vast an area as possible on the northern edge of the
new Spanish territories and gained a reputation for particularly callous acts of
cruelty towards the native Indian peoples who stood in his way. The subsequent
history of San Blas is full of other individuals, just as prominent in their day, of
equally questionable morals.

Over the next two hundred years, other Spanish adventurers and pioneering
clergy pushed the frontiers of New Spain ever further west and north. Expeditions
explored as far away as present-day Canada and Alaska.

Only in 1768 was the town officially founded, as one of a series of towns
planned to support the mighty Spanish Armada in its incursions into the Pacific
Ocean and fights against British and French pirates. The nearby woodlands
promised a seemingly inexhaustible supply of timber for the town's sawmill and
shipyard. Of the boats built in San Blas, perhaps the most important was the
"Princesa", completed in 1778, which made no fewer than eight voyages to the
distant north, more than any other ship.

In the same year the town was established, the Franciscan priest, Junípero Serra set out with boats built in the town to found numerous missions in what was to become California, U.S.A.. San Blas provisioned the new settlements there for years, ensuring a steady flow of flour, tobacco, salt, saddles and other necessities to the north.

The town became the most important naval station on the Pacific coast. Its fine natural harbour was conveniently situated in the lee of a steep-sided isolated hill called the Cerro de San Basilio, once an island whose cliffs had been cut by the

The Bells of San Blas

O n March 12th, 1882, Henry Wadsworth Longfellow wrote his last poem, entitled "The Bells of San Blas". Interestingly, Longfellow had never visited the port, but such was its fame that, as these three verses reveal, he was well able to capture something of its changing importance:

> They are a voice of the Past,
> Of an age that is fading fast,
> Of a power austere and grand;
> When the flag of Spain unfurled
> Its folds o'er this western world,
> And the Priest was lord of the land.

> The chapel that once looked down
> On the little seaport town
> Has crumbled into the dust;
> And on oaken beams below
> The bells swing to and fro,
> And are green with mould and rust.

> ......

> O Bells of San Blas, in vain
> Ye call back the Past again!
> The Past is deaf to your prayer:
> Out of the shadows of night
> The world rolls into light;
> It is daybreak everywhere.

> • • •

sea. On the top of this hill the Spanish built an impressive fortress. Visiting the ruins of this eighteenth century fortress today, it is easy to imagine its significance in colonial times. Its thick stone walls, a massive cistern to hold water, and strategically placed cannons, some of which today point inland, all tell their tale.

On the same hill survive the ruins of the town's oldest church, dedicated to the Virgin of the Sailor's Rosary. Above the main doorway to the church can still be seen two medallions carved in stone, one of Charles III, the other of his consort Doña Josefa Amalia of Saxony. This church is perhaps more widely known in the English-speaking world for having housed the famous bronze "Bells of San Blas", the title of a Longfellow poem.

At the start of the Mexican War of Independence, the port was regularly receiving boats from China and the Philippines bringing silks and spices, and just as often exporting silver, gold, cedar, and salt. Miguel Hidalgo, the independence leader, ordered José María Mercado, priest of Ahualulco, to capture the port, which he did, without needing to fire a shot, on December 1st, 1810. Shortly afterwards, Mercado was on his way back towards Guadalajara with reinforcements for Hidalgo's army when, before they could arrive, Hidalgo was routed at the Battle of Calderón. Mercado pitched his main fire-power (47 cannons) into a deep ravine and raced back to San Blas, pursued by the Royalist leader, General de la Cruz. While making preparations to receive his enemy, Mercado accidentally fell down the precipitous slope below the fortress, and was killed. A statue of Mercado stands in the town's main square.

Following independence in 1821, an Anglo-American trading firm was established, headed by Eustace Barron, the British consul in the state capital, Tepic, and William Forbes, the American consul there. Their import-export firm, Barron, Forbes & Company, was completely unscrupulous. By wholesale bribing of the customs officials in San Blas, they quickly achieved total control over all the port's activities. Only a very small percentage of the cargo traffic through San Blas was properly documented and taxed. The remainder, including British textiles, relabelled as Mexican products on arrival, and silver ingots, passed through as contraband. The company prospered, investing its gains as far north as California and as far south as Ecuador in textiles, banking, mining, agriculture and real estate.

When the State Governor, in 1855, finally decided that enough was enough, and expelled both Barron and Forbes from his jurisdiction, the two men, needing 40 mules to carry their silver, withdrew to Mazatlán from where they enlisted the help of the British Ambassador. The British, somewhat dubiously, claimed that both partners were protected by diplomatic immunity and demanded that they be reinstated as Consuls, which they were.

Later in the nineteenth century, as its port silted up and as the port of Mazatlán further north prospered, trade through San Blas declined and the town's new

Customs House, San Blas

customs house, built three blocks west of the plaza, fell into disuse. Strolling
between its slender columns, bathed in warm, late afternoon sun, who can fail to
relive the building's central role in the vacillating fortunes of Barron, Forbes &
Company? The once proud customs building would make an ideal and appropriate
museum, if it were ever reconstructed.

The San Blas of the mid-nineteenth century was a vibrant and lively place of
more than 30,000 people, three times its present number, many of them recent
arrivals from overseas, bringing with them considerable amounts of capital. Some
of these immigrants later relocated to Guadalajara, marrying and merging into the
wealthy strata of Mexican society. Their resulting investments brought a welcome
revival to these older families, enabling them to diversify their business interests

away from the land, into manufacturing and services, allowing Guadalajara to grow in importance.

Events had conspired for San Blas as a port to fall into the has-been category but Mother Nature played a clever hand and the same silt which had claimed the harbour became the foundation for a network of mangrove swamps, starting a chain of events which has now created a new tourist attraction.

As the dense, interlocking, aerial roots of the mangroves gradually take hold on the soft silt, trapping mud and sediment at every opportunity, the older areas begin to dry out. They became coastal savanna lands, or marismas, with waist-high grass and short bushes. The range of habitats created is a kind of frontier zone between land and sea, harbouring an unrivalled variety of bird and animal life. Representatives of almost half of the 1050 bird species ever recorded in Mexico have, at one time or another, been seen in the immediate environs of San Blas.

The rivers, swamps and canals which remained allowed easy access by boat, and foreign ecotourists began to arrive asking the more knowledgeable local boatmen to take them into the swamps, hoping to catch a glimpse of rare bird species which they could add to their life-lists.

The acknowledged expert of all the birding-boatmen of San Blas is self-taught, English-speaking, Manuel Lomeli. Birders are especially keen to sight the military macaw, the boat-billed heron and the endemic San Blas jay but even non-birders find the sight of diving pelicans, flocks of parrots and the occasional alligator sunning itself on the river-bank a rewarding experience. One of the more popular boat-trips goes through the mangroves to La Tovara, a fresh-water spring which empties into a deep, natural, crystal-clear, bathing pool. A short swim, a beer or two.... What better way to relax?

Only a few minutes drive south from San Blas is Matanchen Bay, a long stretch of firm, golden sand, pristine in the early morning or late evening light. Prior to the founding of San Blas in 1768, this bay had been the port-of-call for the water and supplies needed by the early explorers of the Pacific coast. Once San Blas was established, the bay was abandoned. For those who like swimming in the ocean, the gently shelving sandy beach of Matanchen is perfect.

Further south is Puerto Vallarta, the internationally renowned beach resort, perfect for those who want a beachfront hotel and a few days lazing on the sand. A description of the innumerable sporting and recreational facilities of Puerto Vallarta is beyond the modest scope of this book. Between San Blas and Puerto Vallarta, besides several small but popular bathing beaches such as Guayabitos, is the peninsula Punta de Mita. From the village of the same name, located some 15 kilometres from Highway 200, a co-operative of local fishermen organise short boat trips during the winter months to see dolphins and hump-backed whales swimming in Banderas Bay.

● ● ●

Mexcaltitán

21. Mexcaltitán
Island of Surprises

A short distance north of San Blas is a small island called Mexcaltitán. With barely four thousand inhabitants, it would scarcely be expected to have any real link to Mexico City, the world's greatest metropolis of some twenty million people. But it does, and the link is to be found in the amazing story of the founding in 1325 of the Aztec capital, Tenochtitlan, the city which was later conquered and sacked by the Spanish and rebuilt as Mexico City.

Historians have long wondered about the origins of the Aztec people. There is virtually no evidence of them before they founded the highly organized city of Tenochtitlan in 1325. Clearly such a civilization cannot just have sprung up overnight. So, where did they come from? Aztec legend tells of a long pilgrimage, lasting hundreds of years, from Aztlán, the cradle of their civilisation, a pilgrimage during which they looked for a sign to tell them where to found their new capital and ceremonial centre. The sign they were looking for was an eagle, perched on a cactus. Today, this unlikely combination, with the eagle now devouring a serpent, is a national symbol and appears on the national flag.

In recent years more and more evidence suggests that Aztlán may be far from mythical and that Mexcaltitán, the island in Nayarit, could be its original site.

Ancient codices (pre-Columbian handpainted manuscripts) prove that the Aztecs' search for a new place to live was ordained by Huitzilopichtli, their chief god. It began in about 1111 A.D. when they departed from an island in the middle of a lake. Their two hundred year journey took them through present-day Nayarit, Durango, Zacatecas, Jalisco, Michoacán, Guanajuato and Querétaro, and they may well have rested awhile on encountering familiar-looking islands in the middle of lakes such as Chapala and Pátzcuaro.

One of Huitzilopochtli's alternative names was Mexitli and the current spelling of Mexcaltitán could be interpreted as "Home of Mexitli", or thus, "Home of Huitzilopochtli". In fairness, it should be pointed out that if the original spelling was Metzcaltitán (and "tz" often became transliterated to "x" down the centuries), then the meaning would become "Place next to the home of the Moon".

Whatever the etymology of the name, early codices such as the Boturini Codex show the Aztecs setting out from an Aztlán surrounded by water, in small canoes. The Mendoza Codex, depicting life in Tenochtitlan, has illustrations of similar canoes and in both cases, the canoes and method of propulsion by punting show remarkable similarity to the present-day canoes of Mexcaltitán. Visitors to the island still have to undertake a canoe or *panga* ride to reach the village and it is an intriguing thought that the early Mexicas were doing exactly the same over eight hundred and fifty years ago.

Further evidence comes from an old map of New Spain. Drawn by Ortelius in 1579, it shows Aztlán to be exactly where Mexcaltitán is to be found today, though perhaps at the time this was largely conjecture.

The street plan of Mexcaltitán, best appreciated from the air, is equally fascinating. Two parallel streets cross the oval-shaped island from north to south, and two from east to west, with the modern plaza in the middle, where they intersect. The only other street runs around the island in a circle, parallel to and not far from the water's edge. This street may have been the coastline of the island years ago and may even have been fortified against the invading waters of the rising lake each rainy season. Today, as then, for several months in summer the streets become canals, bounded by the high sidewalks each side and Mexcaltitán becomes Mexico's "mini-Venice" as all travel has to be by canoe.

This street pattern has cosmic significance. It divides the village into four quarters or sectors each representing a cardinal point, reflecting the Mexica's conception of the world. The centre can be identified with the Sun, the giver of all life. The Spanish, as was their custom, built their church there, and today the central plaza with its bandstand is the obvious focal point of the community. Small shops, a billiards hall, the village administrative office and a modern, well-laid out museum complete the central area of the village.

Low houses, of adobe, brick and cement, line the dirt streets and extend right down to the water's edge, in some cases even over the water's edge into the surrounding lake, on stilts. Land on the island is at a premium and, with an ever-growing population, saturation point is very near.

The villagers celebrate one of the most unusual and distinctive fiestas in all of Latin America. On June 29th each year they organise a regatta which consists of a single race between just two canoes, though naturally hundreds of other *pangas* are filled with spectators. One of the competing canoes carries the statue of Saint Peter from the local church, the other carries Saint Paul.

Elaborate preparations precede the race. The village streets are festooned with paper streamers and the two canoes are lavishly decorated by rival families carrying on an age-old tradition. The Ortíz family is responsible for St. Peter's canoe, the Galindo family for St. Paul's. The statues of the two saints are taken from the church and carried in procession to the boats. A pair of punters has previously been chosen from among the young men of the village for each boat. The punters have been suitably fortified for the contest with local delicacies such as steamed fish, shrimp empanadas, and the local speciality, *tlaxtihuile,* a kind of shrimp broth. Each boat, in addition to the punters and the statue of the saint, carries a priest to ensure fair play. The race starts from the middle of the eight kilometre long lake after a short religious service in which the priests bless the lake and pray for abundant shrimp and fish during the coming year. Then surrounding spectator canoes, some with musical bands, and others shooting off fireworks, move aside and the race begins.

Nowadays, St. Peter and St. Paul take it in turns to win, most considerate in view of the violence which years ago marred the post-race celebrations when the race was fought competitively. The ceremonial regatta safely over, land based festivities continue well into the night.

A canoe ride around the island takes about 30 minutes and provides numerous photo opportunities as well as many surprises including a close-up view of the island's only soccer pitch – in the middle of the lake, under half a metre of water. The local children are, of course, expert "watersoccer" players, a fun sport to watch.

Even if you're not interested in the island's past and are unable to see it on fiesta day, your trip to Mexcaltitán will be memorable. This extraordinary island and its village have to be seen to be believed.

To Get There

The island is reached from the Tepic-Mazatlán highway, Highway 15. There are two alternatives. The northern route is signposted 73 kilometres north of Tepic; it starts with 26 kilometres of paved road crossing swampy paddy fields. Then a right turn goes onto 16 kilometres of well-graded dirt road to the landing-stage for boats to the island. The drive is through a naturalist's paradise, teeming with wildlife. The equally scenic southern route begins 57 kilometres from Tepic and is via Santiago Ixcuintla (basic hotels only; don't miss visiting the centre for Huichol Indian culture and crafts) and Sentispac. It leads to the La Batanga landing-stage, and is fully paved.

• • •

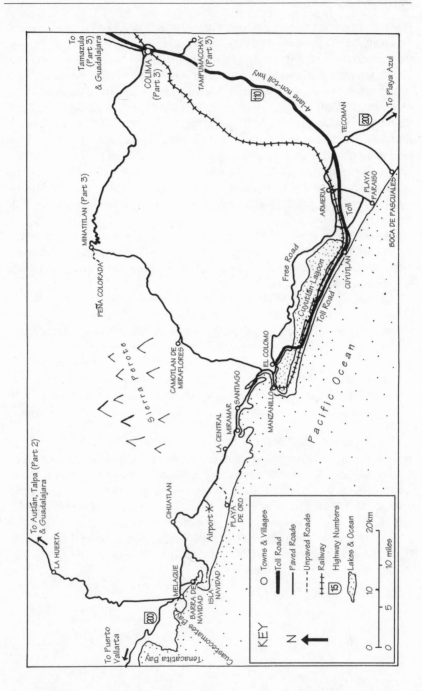

Part Six

22. Barra de Navidad and Melaque
Coastal Jewels

"A beautiful spot on the Pacific. Excellent beaches. Less than a day from Guadalajara by car. Only one very primitive hotel."

Neither the early pirates, nor the modern hoteliers of Barra de Navidad and San Patricio Melaque, twin towns sharing a common bay, can ever have imagined that their favoured watering-hole should be dismissed so simply as in this 1948 tour guide description. Centuries ago, these towns had come alive to the sounds of hammering and sawing, as shipbuilders and buccanneers used the beaches for their headquarters, building vessels to sail as far as the Philippine Islands. Then, for several hundred years, they slept, Rip Van Winkle-like. In the past thirty years they have reawakened, responding to the demands of the Leisure Age, with tourist-related services changing these former sleepy little fishing villages beyond recognition.

Today they offer everything the tourist could possibly require – hotels of every category, excellent restaurants, souvenir shops, discotheques, and water sports. Not surprisingly, they have become a very popular winter hideaway for thousands of well-informed North Americans.

But when does their story begin? At least four hundred and sixty years ago. As early as 1523, the existence of the bay was known to the Spanish explorers in New Spain. What most interested the Spanish was the rumour of an island nearby inhabited only by women, where unlimited numbers of pearls might be found....

The bay at this time was known as Puerto de Xalisco. A few years later, in 1540, the Spanish Viceroy, Antonio de Mendoza, landed in the port on Christmas Day, hence its change of name to Puerto (later Barra) de Navidad.

The port became a centre of maritime activity on the west coast and on November 1st, 1542 a major expedition, captained by Ruy López de Villalobos, set sail

Barra de Navidad Lagoon

with six ships for the newly discovered Philippines, far away across the Pacific.

A few years later, in 1559, a decree from King Philip II of Spain arrived in Mexico, ordering another fleet to sail west to the Philippines. All western Mexico was mobilised in support of this fleet. Roads were built to ferry supplies to Barra de Navidad where the ships were to be built. To this day, the main Guadalajara-Barra de Navidad road is known as The Philippines Way. Food, planks, sails and rigging – all had to be acquired and transported to the port. Every village had to support the effort, which was not without its dangers. For example, the Indians from Ameca complained of "many killed in the transport of rigging to Puerto de la Navidad where they are building boats to go to China." The expedition finally set sail at 3:00 a.m. on the 21st of November, 1564.

Curiously, the expedition's commander, López de Legazpi, kept his sailors in the dark about their true destination until the boats were already well on the way, to prevent any mutiny. In March of 1565 the expedition successfully reached the Philippines, and a new chapter in Spanish colonial history began. No wonder that the Philippines and Mexico share the same unit of currency: the peso. López de Legazpi remained in the Philippines and placed his 17-year-old grandson in charge of finding a way back to Mexico, a feat never previously accomplished. The attempt was successful but when the expedition reached Acapulco in October the crew was so exhausted that no one had the strength to drop the anchor.

This amazing feat of sailing was one of the most expensive explorations of all time, costing more than 350,000 gold pesos. It is commemorated today by a simple monument in Barra de Navidad's small plaza.

For ten years, Barra was a regular port-of-call for Spanish sailors plying the so-called China route between Acapulco and Manila. Then, in 1579, an Englishman, Francis Drake, arrived on the scene.

Drake sacked the small port of Huatulco, now a premier multi-million dollar tourist development in present-day Oaxaca, and attacked the Manila galleon off the coast of California, exposing the vulnerability of Spanish sea traffic. All the west coast ports including Barra de Navidad saw more pirates and corsairs than was good for them in the next forty years.

Then, slowly but surely, the west coast of Mexico with the exception of Acapulco went into a decline, as the centre of colonial operations moved further north into Sinaloa and Baja California.

For centuries, the small port slept....

In the 1950's, San Patricio Melaque and Barra de Navidad were discovered by tourists. Barra de Navidad grew quickly and hotels were built along the narrow, palm-fringed strip of land between the open sea and its inland lagoon.

The town is still small enough to get to know in twenty minutes, yet large enough to have a church and market as well as numerous handicraft and souvenir shops.

The church, dedicated to Saint Anthony, has an interesting crucifix over the altar. When the town was in danger of destruction by Hurricane Lily on September 1st, 1971, and the townsfolk were praying for assistance, the storm suddenly abated; at the same time, the arms of Christ dropped from their accustomed out-stretched position on the cross to hang limply by his side. The disaster was averted and the town has never looked back.

The beachfront walk, paved with pink sandstone and lined by planters and stone benches is very attractive. Strolling along, you can pause and watch brown pelicans diving for fish only a few yards from the immaculately clean beach. Alternatively, gaze upwards and look for the magnificent frigatebirds, with their distinctive forked tails, circling overhead. Stop and bargain with a street vendor for jewelry, onyx wind-chimes, or a brightly coloured *amate* bark-painting. Or just amble along in the warm sunshine, wondering why you don't come here more often.

Both Barra de Navidad and Melaque, round the bay where the swimming is better, have tourist accommodations to suit any budget. Melaque also offers ample RV space for visitors with wheels, at the extreme northern end of the bay. The best spots here are occupied from mid-November through the entire season to Easter, so come early.

Midway along the beach (an easy walking distance) between Melaque and Barra de Navidad is a small lagoon where expert ornithologists have counted, in just a few hours, as many as 75 different bird species, many of them endemic to this region of Mexico.

The much larger, mangrove-fringed lagoon on the landward side of Barra also provides excellent bird-watching. The four-star Cabo Blanco hotel is located here; it has its own marina and is host to an annual deep-sea fishing tourney. On the other side of the lagoon, at its southern end, is the peninsula known as Isla Navidad, a new luxury tourist development with hotel, championship golf course and yacht harbour.

On the shores of the lagoon are several rustic restaurants specialising in seafood; the best are reached only by boat. The local boatmen's co-operative has this part of the action well organised, with fixed (and published) tariffs for every possible trip. Deep-sea fishing expeditions can also be arranged – ask in your hotel for details, or simply wander the streets until someone offers you what you're looking for.

For evening entertainment, the "in-places" are constantly changing but there are always more restaurants, discotheques, and bars in Barra de Navidad and Melaque than any number of tourists could possibly fill.

By road, Barra de Navidad and Melaque are about four and a half hours from Guadalajara. There is relatively little difference in time between the Guadalajara-Colima-Manzanillo super highway with its amazing bridges, continuing northwards from Manzanillo to Barra de Navidad or the more scenic but winding Highway 80, Guadalajara-Autlan-Melaque. The nearest airport is the international Manzanillo airport, only thirty minutes drive to the south.

There are many possible day-trips from Melaque and Barra de Navidad for those seeking a change of pace. To the south, the bustling resort city of Manzanillo (chapter 23) is less than an hour away.

To the north along the Pacific coastline is the area known as the Costalegre, Jalisco's premier coastline, scheduled to undergo major development in the very near future.... At present, the Costalegre is a delightful mixture of sophisticated beach resorts, including a Club-Med village and the charming, secluded, Careyes beachfront hotel, and deserted, white-sand, palm-fringed coves and beaches, just waiting to be discovered.

So be like the pirates of long ago and spend some time exploring Barra de Navidad!

• • •

Manzanillo

23. Manzanillo
The Port of Swaying Fortunes

I n the sixteenth century, when the Spanish adventurer Cortés heard rumours of an exceptionally favourable port site on the west coast of Mexico, he immediately sent men to investigate. Cortés' information came from a Tarascan ruler who, under torture, had told of the arrival at a place called Tzalagua, years before, of the boats of a Chinese mandarin, who wanted to trade with the king of Colimán (today Colima).

Gonzalo de Sandoval was sent to conquer the region for Spain; he found a magnificent port site on a beautiful bay, and reported back that Salagua was an ideal location for ship-building. The mistake over the spelling of the name is understandable since while the Spanish were told "Tzalagua" which meant "place where the cloth is stretched and dried", they naturally understood "Salagua", which in their own language meant "saltwater". Salagua still exists today, between the port of Manzanillo and the tourist area of Santiago.

In 1533, Cortés ordered two ships, the "Concepción" and the "San Lázaro", to be built there. These vessels, commanded by Hernando de Grijalva, were to explore the Mar Bermejo or Gulf of California. In doing so, they discovered the Revillagigedo Islands.

There was almost certainly a small fishing village on the site of present day Manzanillo at that time. The present name is one of the local names for the cohune palm, *Orbignya cohune,* a tall, showy, native Mexican palm which grows along the Pacific shores. This plant should not be confused with either camomile or the highly poisonous manchineel, both of which are known in non-scientific parlance as manzanilla.

A Presidential decree dated the 21st October, 1825, officially established Manzanillo, rather than the silted-up Salagua, as a port for foreign trade. But, for many years, nothing much happened. An English speaking visitor in 1834 was so depressed by the town that he said its most numerous inhabitants were "pelicans and sharks".

Twelve years after opening, because of opposition from Acapulco, San Blas

The Manzanillo-Guadalajara Railway Line

By 1888, railroads had been completed between Mexico City, and Guadalajara, the country's elegant second city, and between Mexico City and the Atlantic ocean port of Veracruz. But the completion of a link from Mexico City to the Pacific, finally achieved via Guadalajara and Colima, was a lot longer in coming....

By the turn of the century there was already a line between Colima and Manzanillo, but this railway terminated in Colima. The Colima-Guadalajara section had still to be started; the first company awarded the concession in 1898, the Central Railroad, ran out of money in 1901. Further delays followed a tragic accident in 1906 when a landslide destroyed a tunnel under construction, killing 17 workers.

The grand celebrations for the inauguration of this line on December 12th, 1908, were among the finest ever seen in Colima. The Mexican President, Porfirio Díaz, attended in person. The State Governor of Colima, also present at the celebrations, was Enrique O. de la Madrid, whose relative Miguel de la Madrid became national President in the 1980's.

The 375 kilometres of track between Guadalajara and Manzanillo are noted for their fine scenery. Guidebook writer and Mexican folkart expert, Francis Toor, wrote that the trip "is through beautiful agricultural and mountainous country with rivers, small lakes, canyons and volcanoes. The people of the villages, who come to the train to sell popular art objects and food, are especially interesting, especially the women of Tuxpan, Jalisco, in their regional dress.... The train... is one of the most exciting trips in Mexico."

The seven-hour rail trip today is still a very pleasant and relaxing, if slow, way of getting from Manzanillo to Guadalajara, or vice-versa. The scenery is just as impressive as it ever was. In 1991, first class train service between the cities was suspended. For years, the eight-hour second class train ride, with 35 stops, has cost just U.S. $3.50 each way – the travel bargain of the century.

• • •

and Mazatlán, Manzanillo was reduced to a cabotage port, one open for local coastal trade only, and not for international traffic. But the following year, because of fears of a French invasion stemming from the Pastry War and possible blockade of larger ports such as Veracruz, it was reopened to guarantee Mexico a lifeline to the rest of the world. Once the French withdrew from Mexico, the port closed again.

In 1846 the U.S. invasion of Mexico and possible renewed blockades of the other larger national ports led to Manzanillo being reopened once more for international business. The U.S. eventually blockaded Manzanillo in January,1848.

Once the Mexico-U.S. war ended, the Mexican President, Peña y Peña, signed the definitive authorization for Manzanillo to become one of the principal ports on the Pacific. This decision gave impetus to the rapid development of inland towns such as Sayula, Zapotlán (Ciudad Guzmán), Tuxcacuesco and Zacoalco, for the production of maize, wheat and soap, all of which were exported in large quantities to California. In 1855, the U.S. opened an agency in Manzanillo, which they elevated to the rank of a consulate in 1860. In general, the period 1850 to 1870 was a time of steady growth for the town.

Perhaps the single most important incident in Manzanillo's nineteenth century history took place in 1857, when Liberal President, Benito Juárez, used the port to escape pursuit from the Conservatives. Juárez and his supporters fled first to Querétaro and then to Guadalajara, but here his army mutinied (they hadn't been paid for months) and he narrowly escaped an assassination attempt. Juárez then fled to Manzanillo via Acatlán (page 77) and boarded a ship bound for Panama. After crossing the isthmus on muleback, he sailed to Veracruz, from where he successfully guided his battered government through crisis after crisis.

Another noteworthy incident from this period was the tragic loss of life which occured on the 27 July 1862 when the U.S. ship "Golden Gate" caught fire and sank at the mouth of the Marabasco river, thirty kilometres west of the port. Some 200 people died in this tragedy and most of the treasure, reputed to be 1.4 million dollars in gold and silver, has never been recovered. At the time, there were no detailed maps of this part of the Pacific coastline but, a year later, Captain G. H. Richards, commander of the British boat "Hecate", made accurate surveys of the harbours of Manzanillo, Santiago, Barra de Navidad and Chamela.

During the decade after 1868, the value of products passing through the port represented almost a third of all the trade on the Pacific coast of Mexico. Only Mazatlán accounted for more. Acapulco was an also-ran, responsible for just 10% of the country's Pacific trade. Manzanillo's population grew rapidly, from 970 in 1868 to 4044 a mere eight years later, and the city has remained an important port, with state-of-the-art installations, ever since.

The port's first lighthouse was built in 1903. Five years later, the completion of the long-delayed railway from Guadalajara to Colima consolidated Manzanillo's position, enabling easy shipment of bulky items between the port and Guadalajara, there connecting with all the country's major railway lines. However, once Southern Pacific extended its track from Tepic to La Quemada in 1927, this boom period came to an end, since it then became possible to send freight from Mexico City to the U.S. border without the need for any ocean transportation.

Manzanillo, the port which took several centuries to grow to maturity, became one of the most interesting and attractive of all Mexico's tourist resorts, combining a thriving, bustling town with magnificent, modern hotels and all manner of sporting facilities.

Each new hotel tries to outdo those built before, but the standard by which Manzanillo's newer hotels are judged is undoubtedly Las Hadas. This Mediter-ranean-style, fully self-contained, super-luxury, top-of-the-market resort has, quite rightly, long had a place in the top ten list of the "World's Leading Hotels". It was conceived by Bolivian tin magnate Antenor Patiño, and constructed on a promontory overlooking Manzanillo Bay. No detail was overlooked. Las Hadas has its own marina, only a few steps from the hotel, and its own golf course, Mantarraya, one of the most challenging in the country. If you're not staying in Las Hadas, it is still well worth visiting, if only to see how the other half lives!

Manzanillo is the self-styled Sailfish Capital of the World. Its annual inter-national fishing tournament, first held in the 1950's, has introduced a sensible set of regulations designed to ensure that fish stocks will never be depleted and hope-fully that the tournament champions can continue to break old records.

It seems almost superfluous to add that there are any number of superb seafood restaurants for you to try or that every conceivable beach and water sport is avail-able somewhere in the tourist zone. There is no shortage of night life, either, with live music and shows in all the top hotels and restaurants.

For those seeking a change of pace, there are many possible day-trips including Colima (chapter 15), Barra de Navidad (chapter 22) and Cuyutlán (chapter 24).

• • •

24. Cuyutlán
Sea, Salt and Sand

"**G**oing southeast from Manzanillo on highway 110 there is a stretch of 27 miles along the ocean and Laguna de Cuyutlán that is one of the most beautiful jungle and coconut forest drives in the world." These words from *Terry's Guide to Mexico* were no exaggeration when they were written in 1965. Other guide-book writers, as we shall see, waxed even more lyrically about the attractions of the Cuyutlán lagoon, the vast swampland to the southeast of Manzanillo, home to an extraordinary variety of wildlife.

The narrow stretch of sand dunes separating the lagoon from the open waters of the Pacific, and once known as The Island, is a natural sand-spit which grew longer and longer northwards, slowly but surely increasing the area of the lagoon behind it. At the end of the last century, this line of dunes became the route of the railway linking Manzanillo to the state capital, Colima. In recent years, it has also been used by the modern toll-highway between the two cities.

But how many motorists speeding along this new highway have any idea of the immense importance the lagoon, to the inland side of the road, played in the history of the state of Colima, and indeed, of a large part of western Mexico?

The Spanish explorers (and conquerors) knew of the lagoon and nearby coastline from the middle of the sixteenth century. The lagoon at this time would have been extremely unhealthy, with clouds of mosquitos flying overhead, and large numbers of caimans swimming about in it. Fevers, malaria included, must have been common. The area would have appeared particularly barren, especially when water levels were low, and a wide expanse of white, infertile salt-flat exposed. But this salt-flat gave the lagoon a considerable economic importance, which had already resulted in various small settlements on its banks.

One of these was called Cuyutlán, a name of uncertain derivation, which may come from "woods of coyules". Coyules are a kind of palm tree, native to this area, which grew on the northern shore of the lagoon on the narrow belt of flat land between the lagoon and the hills.

Salt is first mentioned in connection with Cuyutlán in a document of 1563 when one Rodrigo de Brizuela leaves to his children, Nicolás, Gregorio, Leonor

The Richest Man in Mexico Since Cortés

Pedro Romero de Terreros came to Mexico almost by accident. Born in Cartagena, Spain, in 1710, he came to wind up the estate of a dead brother. In the process, he met an uncle who owned a lucrative freighting business hauling goods by donkey from the port of Veracruz all over Mexico. The uncle died and left so much money to Terreros that he did not know what to do with it. He eventually decided to invest in Real del Monte silver mines.

The persistent Terreros soon became the sole owner, all the other adventurers having dropped out. Doubling the rate of exploration and tunnelling, new ore bodies were discovered.

One of the tunnels was considered such a remarkable feat of engineering that the Viceroy and his Court, dressed in leather coats and caps, together with nobles of the Church, candles in hand, entered its tomb-like darkness to marvel at its size. Terreros extracted from this one mine more than six million ounces of silver and in just twelve years made more than six million dollars clear profit.

Terreros bought and restored several old haciendas including San Francisco Xavier and also built a new, state-of-the-art hacienda called San Miguel Regla which became the family seat.

There was a medieval splendour and munificence about him. He was reputed to be the richest man in Mexico since Cortés. His mines at Pachuca and Real del Monte were the mainstay of the Spanish economy, and after he loaned the Crown a million dollars to help them fight European wars, Charles III rewarded him in 1769 with the hereditary title of the Count of Regla. Terreros also gave the King a man-of-war named "Nuestra Señora de Regla", a magnificent three-decked ship of mahogany and cedar, built in the Havana shipyards and carrying 112 guns. Terreros even boasted that if the King ever came to Mexico, the hooves of his horse would touch nothing but solid silver from Veracruz all the way to Mexico City.

Based on Todd (1977)

• • •

and Bartolomé, not only the salt flats, but also 20 mulattos, 15 negroes and a few other things.... Bartolomé's family became the greatest landowners in Colima history, with properties from the volcano to the sea. They also became early protagonists in the fight to control the salt workings.

Independently, the Viceroy of New Spain gave the entire lagoon to the inhabitants of the town of Colima. The terms of this gift were very vague and caused confusion for centuries. At first, there was no fight between the town and Bartolomé's family over the lagoon; they fished, collected salt, planted cocos, and so on, without getting in each other's way. But, at the beginning of the eighteenth century, the town demanded that the Brizuela family vacate the salt flats, despite the fact that, at the time, another Bartolomé de Brizuela was a member of the town council. In the ensuing power struggle, it emerged that neither side had the right to work the salt since this activity was, by Crown orders, reserved for the Indians. But Bartolomé won the argument and the city had to give him back the areas taken away, and compensation for loss of earnings.

But why all this fuss over some salt?

The commodity had always been considered valuable (the word salary is directly derived from the Latin *sal* = salt) but, in colonial Mexico, its value wasn't only because of its preservative qualities, or for its place in the daily diet. The Spanish had come to Mexico looking for silver and, when they found it, the demand for salt, which was an essential ingredient in the patio process (page 65), grew and was to keep on growing for two hundred years. The process required 68 times as much salt as silver. To put it another way, to produce the 14,250 tonnes of silver obtained between the beginning of the colony in 1521 and the year 1800 required close to one million tonnes of salt.

Given this immense economic importance, the struggle to control the salt flats continued. In 1780, parts of them were bought by Pedro Romero de Terreros, the Count of Regla, who had major interests in silver mines as far away as Real del Monte.

The town council made two more unsuccessful attempts to gain control of the salt workings. Their interests were purely financial: taxes on salt accounted for almost a quarter of the municipal revenue in 1881. In 1873, the Terreros family decided to sell Cuyutlán and this time the salt rights were bought by the Colima State Governor, General Francisco Santa Cruz, who was, naturally, much more able than previous owners to defend himself against the town council.

In April 1879, the General and the town council reached an agreement by which the council renounced any right to claim ownership of the area in the future, and received in exchange 9,200 pesos, to enable them to complete the Government Palace, then under construction.

But a later town council renewed its claims on the land, this time inviting the national President, Francisco Madero, to open a Coastal Exhibition, giving the

Cuyutlán palm groves

townspeople an ideal opportunity to press their claim. The General's wily nephew, also named Francisco, immediately offered the President the use of his private home in Cuyutlán for the occasion and, to give himself increased leverage, donated to the State of Colima sufficient land for founding, legally, the town of Cuyutlán. Though Madero never arrived – he was assassinated first – Cuyutlán now had formal title to the land it occupied.

The end to the dispute over the salt-flats came in 1919 when President Venustianzo Carranza declared that they were national property. Today, several hundred seasonal salt-workers still harvest their annual crop from Cuyutlán lagoon, a lagoon which is now silting up. While a monster thermal electric plant breathes heavily in the background, salt workers still live in houses which have only oil lamps.... The salt warehouse nearest to the railway station has been converted into a small but interesting community museum, explaining the extraction process.

Due to its proximity to Guadalajara, the village of Cuyutlán with its black sand beach became a popular bathing resort. During spring time, the famed "green waves", huge breakers up to ten metres high, excellent for surfing, smash onto the sand. Their colour comes from the mass of marine life and vegetation they stir up as they approach the shore. But other resorts were also built and today Cuyutlán has the air of a decadent, faintly decaying 1940's beach resort, with cheap and comfortable, rather than elegant, hotels.

The drive there from either Manzanillo or Colima still remains very worthwhile. As described by A. t'Serstevens (1960):

"Immediately after Armería you get in touch with the Pacific.... Then you enter the most magnificent forest I have seen anywhere in the course of my wanderings. It is the same fairy like scene we enjoyed at San Blas, but this time, on a much more grandiose scale, a cathedral of a thousand naves, of 100,000 columns, with Gothic vaulting of palms, with emerald glass, and filled with the grey-green, glaucous twilight of submarine grottoes. In the dazzling light when you leave this crepuscular woodland there lies the lagoon ...."

Next time you speed by Cuyutlán on the new super highway, spare a thought for the lagoon's past glory and for those pioneers who braved the mosquitos and the caimans to sustain colonial Mexico's silver production.

To the south between Cuyutlán and Playa Azul in Michoacán are a succession of deserted sandy beaches and rocky headlands, well off the tourist trail and with few hotels or restaurants. These beaches are the breeding grounds of several endangered turtle species who come ashore in winter to lay their eggs .

Anyone wanting to witness this unique sight is advised to do so by joining one of the University of Michoacán or University of Guadalajara-sponsored conservation camps, set up to protect the turtle eggs from indiscriminate poaching. Since few of the other beaches are adequately patrolled, no further details are given here.

• • •

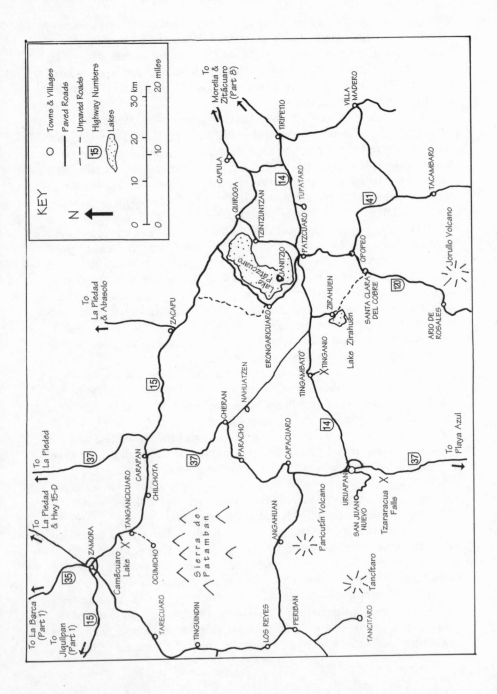

KEY

N

○ Towns & Villages
— Paved Roads
- - - Unpaved Roads
15 Highway Numbers
Lakes

0   10   20   30 km
0   10   20 miles

To La Barca (Part 1)
To Jiquilpan (Part 1)
To La Piedad & Hwy 15-D
To La Piedad
To La Piedad
To La Piedad & Abasolo
To Morelia & Zitácuaro (Part 8)
To Playa Azul

ZAMORA
35
15
37
37
CARAPAN
TANGANCICUARO
CHILCHOTA
OCUMICHO
Camécuaro Lake
TAREQUARO
TINGUINDIN
Sierra de Patamban
LOS REYES
PERIBAN
TANCITARO
Tancítaro
Tzararacua Falls
SAN JUAN NUEVO
URUAPAN
Paricutín Volcano
ANGAHUAN
CAPACUARO
14
PARACHO
CHERAN
NAHUATZEN
TINGAMBATO
TINGANIO
ERONGARICUARO
ZACAPU
15
QUIROGA
CAPULA
TZINTZUNTZAN
Lake Pátzcuaro
JANITZIO
PATZCUARO
14
TUPATARO
TIRIPETIO
VILLA MADERO
TACAMBARO
41
Jorullo Volcano
OPOPEO
SANTA CLARA DEL COBRE
20
ARIO DE ROSALES
ZIRAHUEN
Lake Zirahuén

Part Seven

25. The Road to Tzintzuntzan

T he drive from Guadalajara to the state of Michoacán can either take the federal toll road 15-D or go via Ocotlán and La Barca (chapter 7), following Highway 35 to Zamora. The more scenic alternative, though slightly longer in time, is Highway 15 along the south shore of Lake Chapala (chapter 5), and through Sahuayo and Jiquilpan (chapter 6). All three routes meet in Zamora.

The city of Zamora prides itself on being the strawberry capital of Mexico, a title hotly disputed by Irapuato in the neighbouring state of Guanajuato. One of the charms of this area is that hi-tech machinery and irrigation systems as advanced as anywhere in the world can be seen next to horse-drawn ploughs.

A few kilometres beyond Zamora is the entrance to Camécuaro Park, where graceful cypress and juniper trees shade a clear, cool, lake. The water for this lake comes from a network of springs on the southern side. This is where Princess Atzimba had to take one of her two ritual initiation baths. Today, it is an ideal place for a picnic. There are tables set out around the lake with stalls selling soft drinks and snack foods. Small rowboats can be hired if you feel romantic or energetic.

The main road then continues through various small villages which sell handicrafts, including garish ceramics. The name of one of these villages, Chilchota, which was founded in 1537, means "place where chiles are grown". Chiles were widely cultivated in pre-Columbian times and were paid as tribute from one Indian tribe to another as well as traded with other regions.

At Carapan, Highway 37 from Uruapan joins the road. If you follow the route suggested here for this extended trip into the Michoacán countryside, this is where you will emerge in a few days time. But, for now, continue on via Zacapu and Naranja de Tapia (exquisite painted ceiling in church) to Quiroga, a busy market town with dozens of handicraft stores selling brightly-painted wooden items of every description, from exquisite hand-carved furniture to inexpensive gaudy trinkets. Turn right in Quiroga for the road to Pátzcuaro. Midway between Quiroga

Tzintzuntzan

and Pátzcuaro is the interesting village of Tzintzuntzan.

Tzintzuntzan

Tzintzuntzan has two sixteenth century churches, equally ancient olive trees, a craft market specializing in straw goods and ornaments, plus an archaeological site which was the capital of the not inconsiderable Tarascan empire.

The Tarascans were contempories of the Aztecs, and ruled over an extensive kingdom stretching westwards as far as the shores of Lake Chapala with sporadic contacts into the Sayula lake area. To the east, their territorial limit was very close to present-day Zitácuaro. The Tarascans spoke Purépecha and today the Indians prefer to be called Purépechans; "Tarascan" is more properly reserved for their ancestors and their pre-Columbian empire.

"Tzintzuntzan" is an onomatopoeic Purépecha rendering of the sound made by a hummingbird. The ceremonial centre was still fully active when the Spanish arrived. There were several other Tarascan settlements around the lake including Ihuatzio and Pátzcuaro, where the Tarascan chief or Calzontzi had his summer residence. Most of these Indian villages date from the fourteenth century when Nahuatl-speaking groups first arrived in the region. The oral history of the Tarascans was written down by an anonymous Spanish friar in 1541 forming the basis for most later accounts.

Tarascan buildings were constructed mainly of wood. Only the basements were normally built of stone and today, therefore, it is only these basements or *yácatas* that remain. Some of the cut stones which cover the rubble-filled interiors of the yácatas are ornamented with rock-carvings. The yácatas were rebuilt several times, superimposing the new one over the old, and an archaeologists' trench in the Tzintzuntzan site has been left open to show how this was done.

The scale of earth-moving involved in constructing the temples is remarkable. The entire 425-metre-long platform is man-made. On it were built five yácatas, on the tops of which would have been wooden and thatch structures serving as shrines. The semi-circular shape of these yácatas suggests that they were built to honour the god of the wind, Ik. The Tarascan's ceremonial centre commands a magnificent view over the lake, whose waters would have been lapping at the platform's base during some rainy seasons. The area behind the yácatas, next to the village soccer pitch blazes with colour during the wildflower seasons of late spring and early autumn. The archaeological site has a small, modern museum.

The Tarascans had a mixed economy, collecting fruits and forest products, fishing and practising agriculture, complete with terracing and irrigation. Some archaeologists have argued that many of the pre-Columbian peoples, dependent on the natural world for their immediate survival, were very ecologically-conscious. However, in the Pátzcuaro area, evidence from rates of lake sedimentation now suggests that maybe they weren't quite so environmentally-aware after all. The rates peaked just before the arrival of the Spanish whereas it had previously been assumed that the problem of lake sedimentation had been exacerbated by the twentieth century deforestation of surrounding hills.

The Tarascans made a variety of handicrafts using wood, textiles and lacquer work and were also experts in "feather" art. They probably had specialist carpenters and stone-masons and their polychrome ceramics are amongst the most beautiful of all pre-Columbian America. Employing considerable metallurgical skills, they fashioned jewelry and other small objects out of copper, gold and silver. Their copper handaxes were used as currency throughout MesoAmerica. Examples are on display in the Copper Museum in Santa Clara de Cobre.

It took the Spanish several years to subdue the Tarascans, who were finally defeated in 1528, seven years after the fall of the Aztec capital Tenochtitlan. The torture and murder of the Tarascan chief because he refused to reveal the whereabouts of the tribe's treasures (they didn't have any) incited the Indians to destroy the village of Pátzcuaro.

In retaliation, the Spanish destroyed the Tarascans' temples, carting off many of the stones to build their own churches in their new village. Observant visitors to the beautifully-proportioned patio of the former monastery beside the main church will spot petroglyphs on some of the walls there which betray the stones' earlier placement in the yácatas. This building, decorated with fine old coloured frescoes depicting Franciscan lore, and with parts of its original wooden roof still intact, houses the office of the parish notary and is not always open to the public.

There are other peculiarities here, too, which say much for the realities of sixteenth century Spanish monastic life. When the monastery of Tzintzuntzan was built, two churches were constructed, one for the monks' private use and the other for the lay Third Order. These two churches, only a few steps apart, are about as different as can be, given that they are of similar age. The monks' church, beautifully restored following an arson attack, is light and airy; the Third Order church is dark, gloomy and oppressing. Both, in their own way, are awe-inspiring.

To one side of the Third Order church is a complete-immersion font, shaded by two tall trees. In the large atrium in front of the monastery are a sixteenth century cross and the bent and deformed tree trunks of some of the oldest olive trees in Mexico, brought by special request from Spain for the express purpose of providing the monks with one of their accustomed foods. They are more than four hundred and fifty years old.

Tzintzuntzan's handicraft market is a cornucopia of straw work in every conceivable colour, design and size, which make ideal Christmas decorations or gifts. Also on sale are elaborately carved wooden beams, and examples of the many different local pottery styles including the Ocumicho devil-figures and strange green pineapples as well as finely detailed, hand-embroidered scenes of village life. From Tzintzuntzan it is about twenty minutes drive to Pátzcuaro.

• • •

26. The Multitudinous Attractions of Pátzcuaro

The picturesque town of Pátzcuaro is one of the most fascinating in all of Mexico. It is an ideal place to take visiting family or friends who want to see the "real" Mexico and has dozens of hotels, restaurants and gift shops. If you like the idea of wandering narrow, cobblestone streets, soaking up the atmosphere and smelling the flavours of freshly-cooked snacks in the marketplace, while you keep an eye open for bargains, then stay in the downtown area, which is steeped in history. That way you can walk virtually everywhere.

The town is centred on two plazas, named after famous people who lived in Pátzcuaro in very different centuries. The larger plaza, shaded by magnificent ash trees, commemorates Vasco de Quiroga, the first Bishop of Michoacán. He arrived in the sixteenth century as the Spanish Crown's attempt to rectify the oft-alleged cruelty of Nuño Beltrán de Guzmán, the Spanish conquistador who subdued the local Tarascan Indians. Don Vasco, or *Tata* Vasco as the Indians called him, became a great champion of their cause, helping introduce education alongside religion, and handicrafts alongside fishing and farming. Around this plaza are many superb old buildings including the Palacio Huitziméngari, where the last Tarascan Emperor lived, and the *Casa del Gigante* (House of the Giant).

On the west side of this main plaza is an hotel which was formerly the house where Gertrudis Bocanegra, after whom the second plaza is named, was born in 1765. Of Spanish parentage, she fell in love with a Tarascan soldier named Pedro, to her father's intense displeasure. Pedro and Gertrudis married and together with their ten-year-old son were prominent in the Independence movement. Bocanegra was arrested by the Spanish Royalist authorities and executed in 1817; her husband and son had already died in the fighting.

The second plaza, one block north of the first, has the town market on one side.

Here, bargaining is part of the fun of purchasing inexpensive wooden curios and
woven goods from the wide selection available. On Fridays scores of dark-skinned

The Day of the Dead
– A Mexican Celebration

The indigenous Mexican peoples held many strong beliefs connected
with death; for example that the dead needed the same things as the
living, hence their bodies should be buried with their personal possessions,
sandals and other objects.

With the arrival of the Spanish, the Indians' pagan ideas and customs
were gradually assimilated into the official Catholic calendar. Dead children are remembered on November 1st, All Saints' Day, while deceased
adults are honoured on November 2nd, All Souls' Day. On either day, most
of the activity takes place in the local cemetery.

Children's graves have toys placed upon them and are decorated with
colourful streamers and balloons. Adult graves are more elaborately decorated with offerings of the departed's favourite foods and drinks, candles,
flowers, and even personal items. Brightly coloured Mexican marigolds or
zempasuchitl as the Indians call them, are the traditional flowers used to
guide the spirits home. Unusual art forms which appear only at this time of
year include richly decorated *pan de muerto* (bread of death), skull-shaped
sugar-sweets, and papier mache skeletons.

The graves and altars for the Day of the Dead are prepared by the entire
family who then stand vigil throughout the night to ensure that their dearly
departed recognise close friends or relatives when they come to partake of
the feast offered them. The following day, the spirits presumably having
had their fill, family, friends and neighbours consume what is left. The
village of Janitzio is perhaps the single most famous place for witnessing
Day of the Dead celebrations, but equally interesting observances of the
Day of the Dead are held in many small villages off the usual tourist trail.
In most of these places, the local Indians are uninfluenced and unaffected
by outside contacts.

The magic of the traditional decorated altars can also be appreciated by
visiting one of the replicas constructed in local museums or cultural centres. You will be looking into the dim and distant pre-Columbian past of
Mexico and the Mexican people.

• • •

Indians in traditional dress descend on Pátzcuaro causing the regular market to overflow into nearby streets. These Indians include *curanderos,* herbal medicine practitioners. People come from miles around to consult them about their ailments and be told what herb or combination of herbs will cure them. Walk around the market and take a look for yourself – and, don't be shy – if you're concerned about your asthma or your blood pressure, then ask for their recommendation!

Also on the Gertrudis Bocanegra plaza is the library, housed in the former sixteenth century San Agustín church. The library itself might not be a major tourist attraction, but the mural painted inside it on the far wall certainly is.

The intricate and architectural work of Juan O'Gorman, the Mexican artist responsible for the world's largest mosaic on the wall of the library of the National University in Mexico City, will take your breath away. It tells, in graphic detail, the history of Pátzcuaro and the surrounding area from pre-Columbian times to this century.

O'Gorman painted the mural in 1942 and near the top included an erupting volcano. Little did the artist realise that his mural was prophetic; just one year later, in 1943, and only an hour's drive away from Pátzcuaro, Paricutín volcano emerged in the middle of a farmer's cornfield. O'Gorman's mural portrays the mixing of the Tarascan Indians with the Spanish soldiers and clerics, and the effects, both good and bad, of colonisation and evangelisation. It repays lengthy study.

A short walk from the library to the traffic light and uphill brings you to the Basilica "Nuestra Señora de la Salud" (Our Lady of Health). This impressive church, begun in the sixteenth century, was meant to become the Cathedral of Michoacán, but the plan was considered too grandiose and was suspended. Just inside the door, on the left, the Basilica has a small chapel which houses Don Vasco's remains in well-deserved splendour. Our Lady of Health is a small statuette dating from 1538, made of cornstalk paste and orchid-glue, which is said to have incomparable healing powers.

Only one block south of the Basilica is the Museum of Popular Art, which has fine displays of colonial religious art and local handicrafts from all the villages around Lake Pátzcuaro. At the back of this museum are the remains of a pre-Columbian temple, now the base for a much more modern *troje,* the distinctive wooden house-type of the Purépechan Indians, typical of their heartland area around Cherán and Angahuan, further west. The museum building is a superb example of sixteenth century architecture; it originally housed the Royal College of Saint Nicholas which later became the University of Michoacán.

In the middle of the street in front of the museum's entrance is a covered spring from which water is piped into the town supply. This is the spot where it is said that Vasco de Quiroga, as Bishop of Michoacán, celebrated a mass and prayed for an end to the drought which was affecting the town. At the appropriate moment,

he struck the ground three times with his staff, and water gushed into the air....
Interesting sights await you round every corner. Whatever you do, don't miss
the House of the Eleven Patios. This former eighteenth century convent now
houses weaving and crafts shops, in many of which the artisans patiently continue
their craftsmanship as visitors wander around. The artisans are exceptionally
friendly and always willing to explain what they are doing, or what the difference
is between two apparently identical (but differently priced) pieces of work.
Several shops here specialise in the much coveted lacquer work. Alas, the techniques which were once used for lacquer work are rarely seen today. In the olden
days, such pieces were made by superimposing layers of different coloured
lacquers on a wooden base, and then etching out the design down to the desired
colour, giving a slight relief effect, and making it impossible to achieve very fine
detail in the designs. Today, however, designs are normally painted on. The raw
materials remain the same and include clay, chia oil, and an oily gum made by
cooking plant lice, immersing them alive in boiling water.

Pátzcuaro is a shopper's delight; there are many excellent stores, and an un-
believable variety of desirable items, whatever your budget. Indeed, if you're
about to move to an unfurnished house, you could scarcely do better than invest
in a trip to Pátzcuaro in order to buy everything you might need by way of decorations, furniture, curtains, tablecloths and art work.

There are several islands in Lake Pátzcuaro including Janitzio, inundated at the
beginning of November each year by thousands of tourists eager to witness the
candlelit Day of the Dead ceremonies.

Towering above Janitzio is a monumental statue, of dubious artistic merit, of
the Independence hero, Morelos. The statue was sculpted by Guillermo Ruiz and
is a landmark (some would say eyesore) for miles around. There are murals in its
interior and steps by which one can climb to a lookout point which affords a
glorious view of the lake and its shoreline villages. The island of Janitzio is easily
reached by a regular motor launch service which departs from the pier near Pátzcuaro railway station. The islands in Lake Pátzcuaro may have been temporary
resting places for the Aztecs on their long pilgrimage to found Tenochtitlan.

An even more impressive view is obtained from El Estribo, a volcanic hill just
to the west of Pátzcuaro. A cobblestone road climbs steeply up to a picnic area. On
a clear day, the view encompasses the far shoreline of the lake, as well as numerous
fishing villages and a wide expanse of marshland and former lakebed, now used
for intensive farming of vegetable crops.

Further Afield

Thirty minutes south of Pátzcuaro is the copper working town of Santa Clara
or Villa Escalante. Apart from watching experienced and skilful artisans beating
and shaping the copper items, this is also the best place to buy anything you can
think of made of copper. The town has an interesting small museum, devoted

(what else?) to copper and featuring the prize-winning entries from the National Copper Fair, held here each August. Even the town's bandstand is made of copper. Helpful young boys and the sounds of hammering will help you locate the workshops for a close-up look at the hand-operated bellows which stoke the wood fires used to turn scrap copper into white-hot artifacts.

On the way back from Santa Clara, consider taking the looproad past Zirahuén lake, one of the prettiest small lakes in the country, offering plenty of photo and picnic opportunities. According to local legend, the lake resulted from the tears of a beautiful young Tarascan princess, Zirahuén, who had lost her loved one. Her spirit still lives at the bottom of the lake. Sometimes when a man swims in the lake, she will surface and offer him her everlasting love. If he accepts her offer, the waters will part, together they will walk off into the sunset, and he will never be seen again. The local Indians claim that no woman has ever disappeared whilst swimming in the lake; on the other hand....

Another scenic drive begins near Pátzcuaro's pier and follows the lake shoreline past a trout farm (good food) to Erongarícuaro, known for its painted wooden furniture and fine church; this route eventually completes the full circle of the lake. Several spots along here are first class birdwatching locations. Besides the brilliant-red vermilion flycatcher which you will probably see standing on a fencepost, look also for the dark-coloured northern jacana, a water bird which has striking yellow patches on its wings, egrets, herons and kingfishers.

Traditional Folkloric Dancing

Back in Pátzcuaro in the evening, there are several restaurants and bars, some of which feature live entertainment. One of the "must-see" folkloric spectacles of this region is the Dance of the Old Men, performed on a regular basis in several of Pátzcuaro's top hotels. Very fit and youthful dancers act like decrepit old men, dancing to music called *sones*. No one knows how old the dance is but it

Dance of the Old Men

certainly predates the Spanish Conquest. The dancers are warmly rigged in embroidered white-cotton suits, tunics and wide-rimmed beribboned hats. They wear wooden masks and carry gnarled walking-sticks, an essential prop for their performance. Ask in your hotel for details of where and when they will next dance. The Old Men's Dance is a highlight of many people's stay in Pátzcuaro: consider changing your travel plans in order to see it.

Exceptional Restaurants

For *aficionados* of Mexican food, there are two absolutely outstanding restaurants in the area offering excellent value four-course mid-day *comidas*. Neither of them is well-known to tourists, hence their inclusion here. Next to the gas station in Pátzcuaro, where the highway from Morelia and Quiroga enters the town, is the Camino Real restaurant which has the best chef in Pátzcuaro, bar none. Her Tarascan soup, a local speciality which is a bean-based version of tortilla soup, has to be eaten to be believed. Whatever you choose in this unpretentious restaurant, you will not be disappointed. The Camino Real has a sister restaurant, the Real del Cobre, in Santa Clara del Cobre.

The other recommended restaurant is an hour's drive away, in Tacámbaro. Near the entrance to the town is the Hotel-Restaurant El Molino (The Mill), housed in a museum-piece nineteenth century flour mill, complete with grinding wheels. Simply and artistically decorated and furnished, this restaurant's fixed-price *comida* features slightly finer cuisine than that of the Camino Real, with more subtle sauces and a more varied menu. There is plenty to see in Tacámbaro, and El Molino's comfortable rooms provide accommodation for overnight stays.

From either Tacámbaro or Pátzcuaro it is less than an hour's drive to the city of Morelia, the capital of Michoacán state. Just south of the Pátzcuaro-Morelia highway is the tiny village of Tupátaro, where one of the crown jewels of Mexico's colonial ecclesiastical architecture, a magnificent *artesonado* (painted ceiling), handsomely rewards the detour.

Morelia is a large, bustling city with many historic buildings including Mexico's tallest cathedral, a fine zoo, and smart modern convention facilities in a park which also boasts the state library, planetarium and orchid house. A full description of the many attractions of Morelia, one of the lovelier state capitals in Mexico, can be found in any regular guide book.

• • •

27. To Uruapan via Tingambato
Pyramids and Avocado Groves

Tinganio Archaeological Site

Descending from the mountains, the Pátzcuaro-Uruapan highway enters avocado-growing country at Tingambato. South of the present-day village of Tingambato is the major archaeological site of Tinganio, one of the few sites in Western Mexico where there are genuine pyramids. The site, which dates from about 450 A.D., shows no links to the Tarascans who built Tzintzuntzan.

The site was excavated in 1978 and 1979 by one of Mexico's top archaeologists, Román Piña Chan. It had already been looted by treasure hunters who, however, missed one of Western Mexico's greatest discoveries – an intact tomb full of ceramic offerings and bones.

Piña Chan found that construction at the site could be divided into two periods. During the first, between 450 - 600 A.D., the ceremonial centre took shape. This included an eight metre high eastern pyramid of six superimposed levels and a corresponding western pyramid, partially destroyed by presumed looters. Only the eastern pyramid has so far been restored. Both pyramids have earth cores.

From 600 - 900 A.D., came a change of style to *talud y tablero,* similar to the Teotihuacan architectural style, named after the pyramids outside Mexico City. This style is evident in both the stairway from the main plaza, with its cruciform altar, to the civil area, below which is the tomb, as well as in the ball-court. The ball game was an important ritual, of great spiritual significance, for many Meso-American peoples. The object of the game seems to have been to propel, using hips and back, a hard rubber or stone ball through a high stone hoop. Opinions differ as to whether the losing team or the winning team had the honour of being ceremoniously sacrificed afterwards. This ball court is one of the very few known in Western Mexico, the only region of the country where modern versions of the

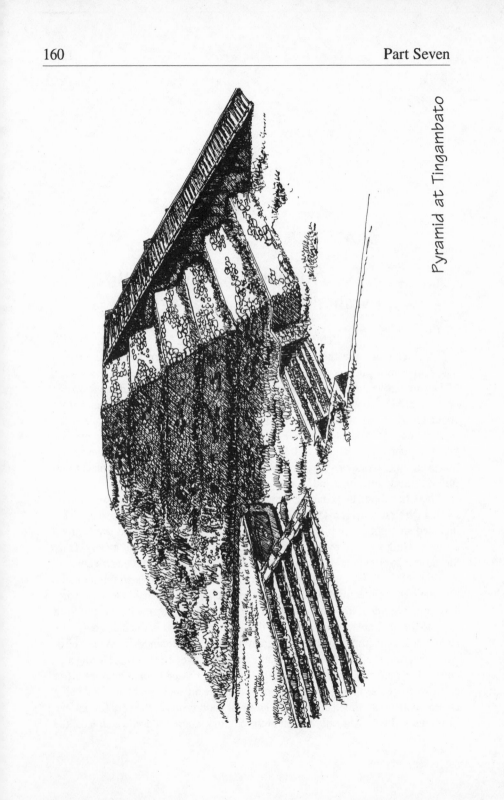

Pyramid at Tingambato

game are still played.

The most sensational discovery in the investigations of Tinganio came on March 8th 1979 when the unlooted tomb was found. Its excavation was dangerous since its roof was in imminent danger of collapse and only one person could work in it at a time. Many bones were recovered but, surprisingly, only one complete skeleton, of a person who had been seated by the entrance. Amongst the many partial skeletons in the tomb were 32 skulls representing all ages and both sexes.

Some of the material had previously been buried elsewhere and had been disinterred for reburial here. Perhaps some important person died and the opportunity was taken to rebury his family or workers? Or maybe the extra skulls were the victims of sacrifices? The mountain of ceramic and other artifacts in the tomb included Pacific Ocean seashells (clear evidence of long-distance trade), snails, small full-body figurines and musical instruments made from shells.

To support this large a ceremonial centre, Tinganio must have had a well-developed agricultural system. Its position between the *tierra templada* (temperate zone) and *tierra caliente* (tropical zone) also made it a natural trading/marketing centre, where the produce of the higher areas such as maize and beans, could be exchanged for that of the lowlands such as cacao beans and tropical fruits.

Tinganio's collapse must have been relatively rapid, since there is no evidence of settlement or building styles after about 900 A.D. There is some evidence that it may have been partially destroyed by fire but, presumably, this alone would not have accounted for its complete abandonment six hundred years before the Spanish arrived.

Uruapan and its National Park

The history of Uruapan, sixty minutes driving time from Pátzcuaro, is intimately connected with wars. Three times in the nineteenth century it served as State capital – during the U.S. invasion of Mexico in 1847, the Reform War in 1859 and lastly, during the war against the French imperialist forces in 1863.

A century earlier, the local people had rebelled against their Spanish masters, refusing to give the Spanish troops billeted in the town any food. An Indian chief was flogged and hundreds of his followers then descended to the town, armed with bows and arrows, shouting, "Die! Die! New Law! New King!". They captured the soldiers and were on the point of executing them when a Franciscan priest intervened saving the soldiers' lives. The Indians may not have killed the Spaniards but they still threw them into the river as a warning for the future.

The river today is a popular place for picnicking and runs through the Eduardo Ruiz National Park. Ruiz was a politician who donated the land to the local council on condition that they pay for most of its upkeep and open it to the public. The nominal admission charge allows you to wander at will along the banks of the Cupatitzio (Singing) River from its very beginning at *Rodilla del Diablo* (Devil's Knee) spring for several kilometres downstream. Natural cascades of water from

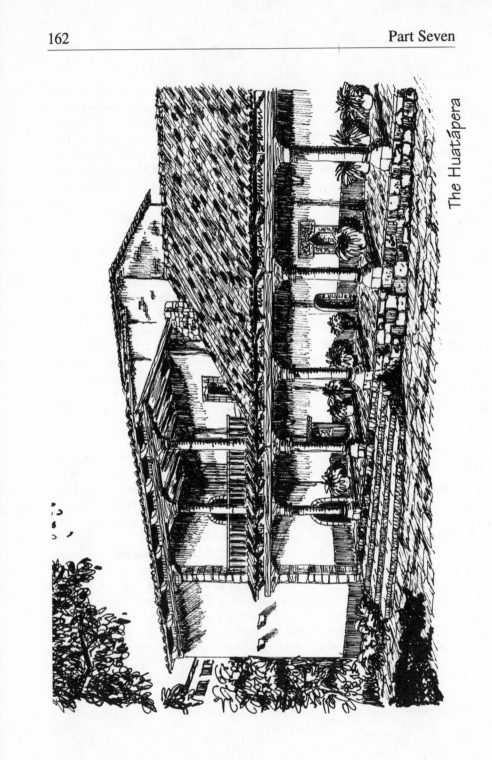

The Huatápera

the river's banks have been artfully complemented by man-made fountains. Strolling in the shade of the luxuriant semi-tropical vegetation, a botanist's delight, provides a refreshing relief from the midday heat. The city's name, incidentally, comes from the Nahuatl for "place of flowers", so visiting this park is a particularly appropriate thing to do.

The luxurious Mansión de Cupatitzio hotel at the northern entrance to the park has one of the best handicraft shops in the entire region, but is certainly not the only hotel in Uruapan worth staying in. The city has a surprisingly large number of good to excellent hotels both on its outskirts and in its centre.

The central plaza of Uruapan, Jardín Morelos, is the hub of the city's commercial activity, much of which has to do with avocado production and marketing. Few old buildings have survived the city's rapid growth in the past fifty years but one which has is the charming sixteenth century Huatápera which was originally both hospital and chapel. The building now houses the Regional Museum of Popular Art with its outstanding collection of early lacquer work, much of it incrusted with gold. This is one of the few places where you can also see a collection of dolls dressed in the many and varied colourful traditional Indian costumes representative of all the regions of Michoacán.

Another historic building worth visiting is the former textile mill, now craft centre, of San Pedro, which dates from the middle of the nineteenth century. It was one of the earliest and largest water-powered mills in the area.

Outside Uruapan

Ten kilometres south of Uruapan, the Cupatitzio river, the river which begins in the National Park and which once powered the mill, flows over the 60-metre high Tzararacua falls. From the car park (take the highway to Playa Azul) it is a steep climb down hundreds of steps to the best viewpoint. Horses can be hired by those who prefer not to trust their own footing. At weekends this park can be very crowded and consequently noisy but during the week it is usually very quiet. Allow at least an hour and a half here if you want to enjoy these spectacular falls. Seeing them you will understand why they are called *el cedazo,* the fishing net.

West of Uruapan, towards San Juan Nuevo, is Jucutacato, a small village where the original of a post-conquest codex, the Lienzo of Jucutacato, now in Mexico City, was once kept. The codex is the oldest surviving document relating the early history of the Tarascan empire by means of a series of pictorial scenes.

San Juan Nuevo (New San Juan) is where many of the villagers evacuated as a result of the eruptions of Paricutín volcano were resettled. It is a spacious, well planned town with wide streets and a strong community spirit. San Juan Nuevo has a gigantic church built to rehouse the patron saint of the Old San Juan church and to commemorate the miraculous survival of the altar there, even as red-hot lava completely surrounded it. The new church has an extensive collection of *retablos* and personal testimonies of people who lost their homes in the eruptions.

• • •

28. Paricutín and Angahuan
A Story-Book Volcano and an Indian Village

The landscape around Paricutín, a volcano which suddenly started erupting in the middle of a farmer's field in 1943, and which stopped equally abruptly in 1952, is some of the finest, easily accessible volcanic scenery in the world. This is a tourist "must-see", even if you can only spare a few hours.

In all of recorded history, scientists have had the opportunity to study very few completely new volcanoes in continental areas (whereas new oceanic island volcanoes are comparitively common) and this is what makes Paricutín so special. The first two new volcanoes formed in the Americas in historic times are just one hundred kilometres apart. The first is Jorullo, which erupted in 1759, and the second is Paricutín.

Dominating the valley where Paricutín now exists is the peak of Tancítaro, the highest point in the state of Michoacan at 3845 metres (12,615 feet), and sometimes snow-capped in winter. In 1943 the local Purépechan Indians inhabited a series of small villages and towns spread over the valley floor. The villages included Angahuan, which still exists today, Paricutín, where 500 people lived, and San Juan Parangaricutiro. The latter was once famous for hand-woven bedspreads and quilts and consequently known as San Juan de las Colchas (bedspreads). Its church, begun in 1555, had never been finished and has only ever had one tower.

On February 20th, 1943, Dionisio Pulido was tending his crops with his wife Paula, their son, and a neighbour when, at four o'clock in the afternoon, they felt the ground shaking under their feet. While they watched, the ground rose more than two metres. Smoke and fine dust rose into the air, accompanied by whistling noises and the smell of sulphur. Sparks set fire to a nearby pine tree. Not surprisingly, they fled.

Angahuan Church

Legend has it that Dionisio first tried to smother the emerging volcano with loose rocks and afterwards was of the opinion that the volcano would never have erupted if he hadn't ploughed his field, but such reports are almost certainly pure fiction.

The volcano grew rapidly, providing onlookers, visiting vulcanologists and residents alike, with spectacular fireworks displays. The month of March was a particularly noisy time in Paricutín's history – explosions were heard as far away as Guanajuato and ash and sand were blown as far as Mexico City and Guadalajara.

A series of lava flows originating from about 10 kilometres underground emerged from the main crater, raising the volcano's height to more than 400 metres before its first birthday. In early 1944, another lava flow streamed in a gigantic arc reaching the outskirts of the town of San Juan Parangaricutiro. Fortunately, the town had already been abandoned. The parts of the church which survived in "old" San Juan, including its altar, can still be visited today, though reaching them involves clambering over jagged blocks of lava.

The village of Paricutín also had to be abandoned before the relentless flow of lava overwhelmed it. In the case of this village, however, nothing was left. A small cross atop the lava marks its approximate position. The evacuated villagers were escorted to Uruapan by soldiers, and later founded San Juan Nuevo (page 163). Other villagers settled in already existing towns and cities.

Suddenly, in February 1952, nine years after the volcano first erupted, the lava stopped flowing. In many places, plumes of hot steam still rise from the ground, ground that is still most distinctly warm to the touch.

Enjoying a full day at Paricutín has been made much easier since the construction of rustic tourist cabins on the edge of Angahuan village. The restaurant, which serves tasty local specialities, gives clients a panoramic view encompassing the lava and the half-buried church. In February 1993, to commemorate the 50th anniversary of the volcano, a permanent exhibition was inaugurated of maps, charts and photographs describing the volcano's history and the surrounding area.

Horses can be hired for a trip to the church or to the more distant cone of the volcano. The latter requires an early start since the last part involves clambering up the loose ashes and cinders which comprise the cone and scrambling onto the narrow rim of the truly magnificent crater. A marvellous view can be enjoyed from atop the crater rim and only then can the full extent of the area devastated by the volcano be fully appreciated. Nothing can quite have prepared you for this startling lunar-like landscape.

Angahuan Village

Angahuan, the nearest village to the volcano, is fascinating in its own right, with a lovely mid-sixteenth century church with many Moorish characteristics, peculiar and distinctive house styles which make widespread use of local timber and an array of hand-made woollen items.

The original name was Andanhuan, which the Indians say the Spanish couldn't manage to pronounce, hence its transformation to Angahuan. The Purépecha name meant "place on high where people stopped" or "place where the person on high (captain) stopped".

The Spanish, complete with captain, arrived in 1527, under the command of Nuño Beltrán de Guzmán. One of the first missionaries here, Jacobo Daciano, ordered a Moorish stone-mason who was with him, to stay in Angahuan and build a convent. The mason did a fine job – look closely at the church ceiling – and Angahuan church is one of the very few in the country with such marked Moorish influences. The church is dedicated to *Santiago* (Saint James) and, as elsewhere in Mexico, he is shown astride a horse.

Across the small plaza is a wooden door richly carved in a series of panels which depict the story, or at least one version of it, of the eruption of Paricutín. One panel shows that the artist, Simón Lázaro Jiménez, clearly had a sense of humour about tourism. His design won first prize in a regional handicraft competition in 1981. The artist rejected the prize, copyrighted his unusual design, and used the finished handiwork as his own front door.

Dr. Atl and Paricutín

One of Mexico's more extraordinary turn-of-the-century individuals, Gerardo Murrillo (Dr. Atl), artist, vulcanologist, explorer, muralist and writer, arrived soon after Paricutín began activity and lived on its slopes for several months. In 1950, Atl, the Father of the Mexican artistic revolution and the mural movement, published a magnificent, scholarly account of the volcano's activity, illustrated with more than a hundred drawings, maps and photographs.

Atl was a fervent suporter of those Indians who didn't want to be moved from their homes as the lava advanced upon them, and told many stories of his own narrow escapes. Once, an Indian woman nearby lost her house to the lava, but saved a hen and a saucepan – calmly setting to work cooking it and offering Atl a share in her meal.

On another occasion, Atl resigned himself to death as lava virtually encircled his small campsite. He ran to his tent and salvaged a machete and a bottle of whisky, just as the lava finally stopped. Atl claimed afterwards that he threw the machete into the lava because it was useless but that the whisky had been just sufficient to revive him!

Atl eventually died, aged 89, in 1964. His dramatic and exciting paintings of Mexico's volcanoes have never been equalled.

• • •

Many small Mexican towns and villages rely on a village loudspeaker system for relaying all important events and news. Angahuan is no exception; look for the speakers mounted high over the plaza. Local announcements are in Purépecha, the local Indian language totally unintelligible to Spanish speakers. This is the only common language for the Indians in this area, since many of them don't speak Spanish – their children will often translate for them. The Purépecha language is not closely linked to any other native Mexican language, but is distantly related to that spoken by the Zuni of the U.S.A. and the Quechua and Aymara of South America.

The distinctive house-types of Angahuan called *trojes,* built of wooden beams with steep roofs, are slowly giving way to modern monstrosities built with concrete blocks. The roofs with two slopes, one each side of the house, are called "two waters", those with four slopes "four waters".

From Angahuan, the highway back towards Carapan passes through Paracho and Cherán. Paracho is Mexico's guitar-making centre where stringed instruments of all kinds, and all prices, have been made for hundreds of years. This is also a good place to look for wooden toys and miniatures. The next town, Cherán, is so typically Indian that it even has a radio station broadcasting in the Purépecha language.

• • •

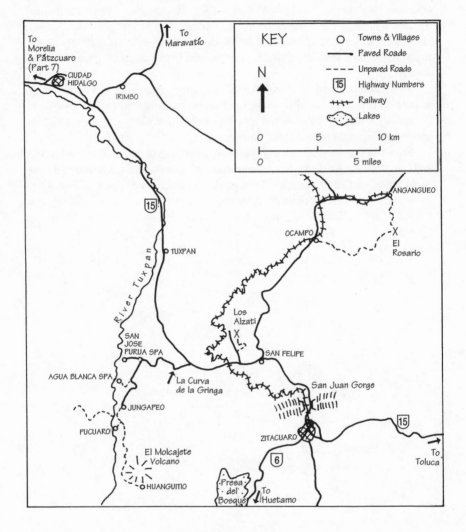

To
Morelia
& Pátzcuaro
(Part 7)

To
Maravatío

KEY

N

○   Towns & Villages
── Paved Roads
--- Unpaved Roads
[15] Highway Numbers
+++ Railway
Lakes

0   5   10 km

0   5 miles

CIUDAD
HIDALGO

IRIMBO

[15]

ANGANGUEO

OCAMPO

X
El
Rosario

River Tuxpan

TUXPAN

Los
Alzati
X

SAN
JOSE
PURUA SPA

SAN FELIPE

AGUA BLANCA SPA

La Curva
de la Gringa

San Juan Gorge

JUNGAPEO

PUCUARO

ZITACUARO

[15]

To
Toluca

El Molcajete
Volcano

[6]

HUANGUITIO

Presa
del
Bosque

To
Huetamo

Part Eight

29. Butterflies by the Million
The Monarchs of Michoacán

E very winter, some one hundred million monarch butterflies fly into Mexico from the U.S. and Canada. On arrival they congregate in a dozen localities high in the temperate pine and fir forests of the state of Michoacán. As a species, monarchs are native to North América, but subsequently island-hopped their way around the world – across the Pacific to Hawaii, Tonga, Samoa, Australia and New Zealand, and across the Atlantic to Europe. Most monarch butterflies never migrate, but a large part of the North American monarch population undertakes an annual, long-distance migration, a journey without parallel in the insect world.

Scientists are still unable to explain all the details of this enigmatic annual migration. How is it, for example, that the butterflies returning to Mexico, four or five generations down the line from those who flew north in April, manage to find exactly the same groves of trees as their ancestors, high in the Mexican mountains? Is their unexpectedly sophisticated navigational ability due to gravitational differences, an incredible innate accuracy in pinpointing position by measuring the angles of the sun's rays, or due to the effects of magnetism in underlying rocks?

The latter theory is perhaps the most likely since the areas of Michoacán chosen by the butterflies for winter residence all lie along Mexico's Volcanic Axis, where various magnetic minerals are abundant. The exact sites where the butterflies overwinter were only found in the mid 1970's after a search of nearly forty years.

Surprisingly, their numbers are not severely depleted by predatory animals and birds during their three to four month somnolence on Mexican fir trees. In flight, their bright orange and black wings act as a warning, signifying danger, to birds. At rest, only the undersides of their wings are exposed; the resulting grey and white pattern is excellent camouflage so long as the butterflies remain on the trees.

Furthermore, the monarch larvae feed on milkweed plants (*Asclepias spp.*) Most of these plants are poisonous to almost all animals, but *Danaus plexippus,* to give the monarch its scientific name, can digest them and its larvae retain the milkweed's cardenaloid poison. The resulting adult butterflies are sufficiently

Why Do Butterflies Feature So Prominently in Pre-Hispanic Mythology?

Pre-Columbian Indians had many strongly held beliefs and ideas about butterflies, presumably because they recognized their vital role in the pollination of the plants and crops on which they depended for food.

Some believed the butterflies represented the seed or blood of the sun. Another legend says that the sun from its mid-day zenith is carried westwards daily by the Cihuateteo, the souls of women who died in childbirth. When the sun sets once again into the underworld, the Cihuateteo are transformed into divine, and therefore inedible, butterflies, remaining in Western Mexico. The butterflies' sharing of the Gods' divinity made it impossible for birds to eat them. This same legend also relates that the sun is carried from sunrise to its zenith by the souls of warriors who died in battle – at the zenith as they hand over to the Cihuateteo, these souls are transformed into hummingbirds, and fly east.

There are many other butterfly-related beliefs. The symbol of the fifth sun in Nahuatl cosmology is Naui-Olin, often depicted in the shape of a butterfly. The insects are also associated with Xochiquetzalli, the multifaceted goddess of flowers and dance, counsellor of pregnant women, and patron of painters, weavers, silversmiths and practitioners of feathered art.

Butterflies are also linked to the gods of travel: Zacatontli, "Little Grass" and Tlacotantli, "Little Twig". In their honour, and to this day, travelling merchants often cut butterfly shapes out of paper before beginning a journey.

There are many designs and frescoes dating from pre-Aztec times which depict butterflies. Perhaps the most famous are the Tetitla frescoes in Teotihuacan. There are other butterfly designs in Xochicalco. Across the country there are countless placenames which include the linguistic element, *papalotl*, butterfly.

• • •

venemous to deter would-be predators after their first mouthful. Only some mice, orioles and a few other species of birds have any degree of immunity to milkweed poison. Some other non-poisonous butterfly species have wing designs and colours which closely mimic the monarchs, providing them also with some protection against potential predators.

The tagging of butterflies has proven that they make the 2500 kilometre trip each way at an impressive average speed of 20 km/h, with maximum speeds of up to 40 km/h. Monarchs don't fly at night, partly because their wings need sunlight to act as miniature solar-panels, raising their body temperatures as much as 10 to15°C above ambient air temperatures.

One third of their dry body weight is energy-giving fat but far from losing weight on their exhausting journey south, they actually appear to gain it!

There are still many mysteries about the monarchs but they certainly provide one of the most amazing natural spectacles to be seen anywhere on earth. Millions of orange butterflies, with black and white-spotted wings, whether flying overhead or, as on cooler days, clinging apparently lifeless to the grey-green fir trees in such numbers that the trees appear to be in blossom, are an absolutely unforgettable sight.

In September and October, as temperatures in the U.S.A. and Canada fall, and food supplies become scarce, the monarchs fly south in small groups. Some of these groups fly only as far as Florida or western California where they spend their winters in milder conditions. But many of the small groups from east of the Continental Divide eventually coalesce and fly much further south, as far as Mexico, arriving en masse in the state of Michoacán towards the end of November. This migratory group is comprised of as many as 120 million individuals and spends the winter in semi-dormancy, on the pine and sacred fir (*Abies religiosa*) trees found at altitudes of about 3050 metres (10,000 ft) along Mexico's central Volcanic Axis. Until spring comes, in March or April, these butterflies cling to the branches and trunks of the trees, enjoying temperatures between 10 and 16°C, protected from cold northerly winds. Their metabolism slows down in these low temperature, low oxygen conditions and they exhibit movement only on warm, sunny, days.

The generation that flies into Mexico does not mature sexually until the following spring. In February and March, the best months to see them, early spring sunlight begins to penetrate the groves of fir trees, temperatures begin to rise and the forest floor slowly comes alive with new plant growth. The butterflies, having successfully overwintered the worst weather, unfurl their wings and flutter about in search of food and water. As they regain their strength, so they become sexually mature and the mating process starts.

After mating, the butterflies begin to leave the reserves, flying back towards the north. Five days later in northern Mexico and the southern U.S.A., each female lays two to three hundred eggs on the underside of milkweed leaves. They first check, by smell and touch, that no eggs have already been laid there, and then space their eggs in such a way so as to ensure that each larva that hatches two to three days later will have an adequate supply of food. The larvae grow quickly, changing their skins five times before becoming pupae. After a further two weeks, butterflies emerge, and the whole cycle begins once more. Each generation of monarchs probably acquires a different chemical "blueprint", based on the exact species of milkweed it eats, giving it the information it needs to know where to fly.

The succeeding generations continue flying northwards, back to the U.S.A. and Canada, arriving in April. It is unlikely that any individual butterfly successfully completes the entire 5000 kilometre round trip. Most of those who fly south die soon after mating in spring, while those who head north cannot hope to survive long into the summer, when normal reproductive cycles, each lasting from four to six weeks, are reestablished. The last generation of each summer, perhaps prompted by shorter days, soon departs on the next wave of mass migration to Mexico. Some of them will cross the Great Lakes on their return. They have been spotted flying south at heights up to 1,500 metres and exploit thermals to gain height and save energy.

While the species as a whole is in no danger of extinction, the migratory group is under considerable threat from both climatic extremes and human activity. Unusually cold spells and hailstorms have sometimes caused the loss of millions of butterfly lives, though without, as yet, any discernible effect on total monarch numbers or its migration. Human activity has greatly reduced the area of the monarchs' natural habitats, in both California, by real estate developments, and in Michoacán, by forest clearance for timber and agriculture.

The Mexican conservation programme for the butterflies is designed to provide alternative sources of revenue and employment for local *campesinos* who depend on the land and forest for their livelihood. After some doubtful years in the early 1980's, there is now a concerted conservation effort to prevent further destruction of the monarchs' unique habitat.

The modest entrance fees help to fund development projects in the local communities. There is a strict code of conduct for tourists who must sign a visitors' book and obey the rules: no smoking, litter, running, noise or straying from the well-marked paths, and above all, no collecting of specimens.

The new rules have worked but it is still preferable to avoid going at a weekend when the reserve is at its busiest. It is far more pleasant to go during the week – then you can appreciate the marvels of nature in the company, not of hundreds of people, but rather of millions of butterflies. Standing still for a few minutes in the quiet of the forest to get your breath back on the way up the trail, you will be just as surprised as I first was when you realise that the gentle swishing sound you can hear when the birds aren't singing, isn't the sound of the wind blowing through the tree tops but the sound caused by millions of tiny wings beating as the butterflies flutter about in the sky.

The most accessible reserve open to the public is El Rosario, where there are dozens of souvenir stalls and rustic snack stands – don't miss sampling the delicious hand-made blue-corn tortillas – and an exhibit on the monarchs' life-span and annual migration.

The narrow trails within the sanctuary, with information boards at regular intervals, wind steeply several hundred metres uphill, reaching a maximum altitude of 3050 metres. This altitude can cause some shortage of breath and air temperatures are generally low, so bring a sweater.

Anyone driving their own vehicle to El Rosario is advised to use the route via San Felipe on Highway 15 and Ocampo. The San Felipe-Ocampo junction is marked by a line of fruit and soft-drink stalls, many of which in season sell delicious *granadas* (pomegranates). Also at this junction there is an interesting sixteenth century church which, until as recently as 1995, had tombstones in its atrium, unusual in Mexico. Normally, the Spanish buried their dead as far away from the churchyard as possible, presumably to avoid the risk of disease.

It is only fourteen kilometres from San Felipe to Ocampo, from where any vehicle with adequate ground clearance, including the local taxis, can negotiate the fourteen kilometres of dirt road to the sanctuary car-park. Hikers, however, may prefer to use the more direct but steeper approach from Angangueo.

• • •

Angangueo

30. More Treasures of the Sierra Madre

There are many places of considerable appeal near the El Rosario reserve which make it desirable to spend several days in the area if you possibly can, even if it's not butterfly season.

Angangueo

A few minutes north-east of Ocampo is Angangueo, a typical Mexican silver-mining town. At the entrance to the town are strange, step-sided earth mounds – these are not pre-Columbian pyramids but twentieth century spoil-tips.

Angangueo's pretty single-storey buildings with red roofs and flower-filled porches line a narrow main street which gradually meanders up to the head of the valley and the town plaza. There are two large churches on this plaza, an obvious sign of the town's former wealth. Worth visiting, one block uphill from the plaza, is the former residence of Bill Parker, 1930's mine superintendent, and his wife Joyce, a keen photographer. Mining in Angangueo declined after a serious accident in 1953, said to have been caused by the company's foreign management in response to a threatened strike. The miners who lost their lives in this accident are commemorated by a huge statue which overlooks the town.

The hustle and bustle of industrial activity has been replaced by a slower, more leisurely approach to life. In Angangueo, afternoon siestas are still the norm; don't expect the small stores to reopen at any particular time in the afternoon.

Railway enthusiasts will appreciate not only the standard-gauge mainline and its end-of-the-line station which squeezes the town's main street against the valley side but also the narrow-gauge mining track which burrows deep into the hillsides.

Zitácuaro

For those who prefer bigger, more cosmopolitan cities, the nearest is Zitácuaro, nine kilometres east of San Felipe. Just before entering the city the road crosses a modern, concrete bridge. Pull off the road at this point and, assuming you have a good head for heights, and entirely at your own risk, walk onto the nearby railway

Agua Blanca

bridge (not many trains come this way each day) for a truly staggering view down between the sleepers, or ties. Far, far, far below you, the San Juan river rushes through this amazingly narrow, precipitous, and totally unexpected chasm.

Zitácuaro is bypassed by most non-Mexican tourists who, failing to discover a single souvenir shop, don't stay long enough to find the good hotels and restaurants that the city has. In and around the city are several places worth seeking out.

Only a few hundred metres from the freeway is a gorgeous, vintage, railway station, a classic of European design. The city has very few old buildings. A succession of bloody battles all but destroyed the entire city on several occasions. The bravery shown by the inhabitants during the War of Independence and the French Intervention resulted in the city being awarded the official pre-name "Heroica". Almost all major Mexican cities have a church on their central plaza. Zitácuaro doesn't. It does, however, have the customary mural depicting local history in the city hall.

Diana Kennedy, internationally famous for her cookbooks on Mexican cuisine, has long made her home just outside Zitácuaro, close to the Rancho San Cayetano, a small, exclusive hotel on the road towards Huetamo and the Del Bosque reservoir. The San Cayetano's charm lies not only in its comfortable rooms but also in its first rate cuisine. What better recommendation for the food here could there be than Diana Kennedy regularly bringing friends to dine in the hotel?

Slightly further afield, west of San Felipe, are several other worthwhile places to visit, including a major archaeological site.

The Los Alzati Archeologial Site

The mounds outside Angangueo may not be genuine pyramids, but the ones at Los Alzati certainly are. The pyramid is signposted opposite the large Resistol chipboard factory on Highway 15, two kilometres west of San Felipe.

Visitors to the monarch butterflies never imagine that they may be treading in the thousand year old footsteps of Matlatzinca Indians. But researchers have suggested that these Indians knew about the monarchs' migration and even constructed a monumental pyramid in nearby Los Altzati which served, in part, to celebrate their annual autumnal arrival.

The site, covering more than twenty hectares, was also constructed to fulfil the Matlatzinca's military objectives. Forgotten after the Spanish conquest, it was rediscovered by a *campesino* in 1962. The ceremonial centre is dominated by one of the biggest pyramids in all of Mexico, almost eighty metres (250 feet) high. From the top, an incredible panoramic view stretches clear across the green Zitácuaro valley. It is an especially thought-provoking scene at sunset as long shadows spread slowly over the landscape, throwing the relief into sharp perspective.

At its peak in about 800 A.D., the site was home to as many as 25,000 Matlatzincas. Architecturally, the principal influences are from Teotihuacan. Many petroglyphs have been found here including clear representations of land snails, a human foot and deer.

The earliest evidence of settlement in the area dates from 200 B.C. when the Indians lived by subsistence agriculture, perhaps with some irrigation from local springs. By 650 A.D., irrigated agriculture was well organised. Then a natural extension of the nearby volcanic slope was enlarged and reinforced with stonework to construct a flat base for the main ceremonial structures. Despite grave-robbers' diggings, there is no suggestion that this site ever concealed any tomb or treasure.

The site shows clear evidence of having been reconstructed several times, perhaps every 52 years in accordance with native Meso-American cosmology. For unknown reasons the site declined in importance after 900 A.D. and after that no more rebuilding was carried out.

The Gringa's Curve

Further west along Highway 15, in the midst of stunning scenery, is the road for Jungapeo. To movie-goers, this is classic *Treasure of The Sierra Madre* country. It comes as no surprise, then, to discover that much of the film was shot in this area.

The first bend on the narrow road to Jungapeo has the unique distinction of being the only bend on a minor road to be specifically named on a Mexican survey map – La Curva de la Gringa (the Female Gringo's curve). Imaginative interpretations of the origin of this name abound but the local version is that only days after this road was first paved in the 1950's, an American lady driving an oversized "gas-guzzler" down to the then luxury spa of San José Purúa, completely missed the bend and ploughed into the cornfield, surprised but otherwise none the worse for wear. The locals christened the dramatic 110-degree bend "La Curva de la Gringa" and so it remains.

The Agua Blanca – A Simple, Relaxing Spa

Past the San José Purúa entrance and off the Jungapeo road to the right is the driveway to the Agua Blanca spa-hotel. Many butterfly visitors, after the cool and dusty atmosphere in the fir forests want nothing more than a long soak in a warm tub and this is the ideal place.

The hotel, built in the 1940's, has charming Purépecha Indian style rooms arranged around three sides of the greenest lawn in Mexico. Don Enrique and his staff are genuinely helpful and the family atmosphere of this get-away-from-it-all hotel is hard to beat. There is ample evidence that the thermal springs of the upper Tuxpan River, which flows through the Agua Blanca's grounds, were revered as medicinal and relaxing by the pre-Columbian Tarascan emperors. The Royal household used the nearby springs as thermal baths. When the Spanish arrived, they heard stories of the "Fountains of Youth", and not surprisingly, set out to verify them. Ponce de León, one of the Spanish conquistadors, tried hard to persuade the Indians that they should reveal the fountains' location to him – but they misled him into continuing northwards, as far as modern-day Florida, on his futile quest.

The waters of the hotel pools are 32°C, warm rather than hot, and contain a rich and healthy chemical cocktail of carbonates, bicarbonates, chlorides, silicates and sulphates. Their slight radioactivity is said to assist in alleviating muscle, joint and intestinal disorders.

The hotel grounds contain a magnificent pot-pourri of endemic and exotic plant species, including Dutchman's pipe on a wall near the entrance, an orchid tree, coffee, mamey, blue-flowering jacarandas and distinctive white-barked *amate* or wild-fig trees (the source of the bark paper used in Mexican handicrafts), whose roots hold tenaciously to the bare rock on the slope overlooking the river Tuxpan.

Also inside the grounds is the romantically-named Bridal Cascade, a 25-metre waterfall which splashes onto the huge leaves of banana plants growing on the bottom of a narrow gorge. The black-and-yellow striped butterflies which can usually be seen fluttering about here are called, perhaps not surprisingly, zebra butterflies. They are a tropical species and at dusk form large roosts hanging from twigs and branches, invisible unless you know exactly where to look.

On the slope between the hotel pools and the River Tuxpan are unusual rock formations and caves. These grottos, though they look as though they should be in limestone, and though their interior formations resemble stalactites and stalagmites, are in fact in lavas, and the formations are mostly siliceous, presumably deposited from the warm ground-water. Such features are quite unusual on a world scale since silica is virtually insoluble except in warm water. The grottos started life as lava caves and the siliceous "stalactites" were added later.

Superb View

Further downstream in the Tuxpan valley are several examples of geologically recent cinder cones, 100 to 300 metres high. From Jungapeo, an unpaved road follows the eastern side of the valley. After two kilometres, a track to the right leads to the ruins of Púcuaro, an ex-hacienda. Still further down the valley, the small village of Huanguitío lies at the edge of a wide, flat, and fertile river terrace which is intensively cultivated for semi-tropical produce, including bananas and tomatoes. It is built exactly on a spring line in the underlying limestone. Water cascades down the slippery rocks forming a small pool beside the road, used by the villagers as a source of fresh-water and a natural wash-tub.

Rising above Huanguitio are the steep, cindery slopes of El Molcajete volcano. El Molcajete, a name very common in central Mexico, means pestle, as in pestle and mortar. It derives, of course, from the bowl-shape of the volcano's crater. The view from the rim of the crater of this particular El Molcajete volcano, reached after an hour's climb from the village, is exceptional, one of the finest anywhere in Western Mexico.

• • •

Table of Altitudes and Approximate Driving Times (hrs:min)

Altitude Metres	Altitude Feet	Town/City	Chapala	Colima	Guadalajara	Manzanillo	Morelia	Puerto Vallarta
1910	6260	Aguascalientes	4:05	5:45	3:25	7:00	4:45	8:50
1000	3280	Autlán	2:50	2:15	2:30	2:25	7:20	4:55
3	10	Barra de Navidad	4:30	1:55	4:10	0:45	7:55	3:15
1525	5000	Chapala	-	2:30	0:40	3:35	4:15	5:40
460	1500	Colima	2:30	-	2:10	1:15	5:55	5:10
1570	5140	Guadalajara	0:40	2:10	-	3:25	4:35	5:20
1650	5430	Jiquilpan	1:55	2:50	2:15	4:05	3:15	7:15
1940	6370	Lagos de Moreno	3:25	5:15	2:45	6:30	4:05	8:20
3	10	Manzanillo	3:45	1:15	3:25	-	7:10	3:55
2250	7380	Mazamitla	1:45	1:50	2:05	3:05	4:05	7:00
1940	6370	Morelia	4:15	5:55	4:35	7:10	-	9:45
2170	7130	Pátzcuaro	4:00	5:20	4:20	6:35	0:50	9:30
3	10	Puerto Vallarta	5:40	5:10	5:20	3:55	9:55	-
4	13	San Blas	4:55	6:25	4:15	7:30	8:40	3:10
1040	3410	Talpa	3:40	4:15	3:35	4:50	8:00	*3:00
2080	6825	Tapalpa	2:40	1:50	2:20	3:05	6:15	7:30
915	3000	Tepic	4:10	5:30	3:30	6:45	8:10	2:15
1220	4000	Tequila	1:40	3:10	1:00	4:25	5:35	4:20
1570	5140	Zamora	2:00	3:50	2:10	4:45	2:15	7:30
1780	5840	Zitácuaro	6:30	8:10	6:40	9:25	2:20	11:40

* dirt road

On Maps and Asking Directions

S tories abound of tourists being hopelessly misdirected after asking for directions in Mexico; some are undoubtedly true, others apocryphal. This is partly because most Mexicans do not use maps frequently and partly because new roads and renamed streets quickly render old maps out-of-date.

Not surprisingly, tourists find it difficult to understand why they are smilingly told that the place they are looking for is "only two blocks further on" when in reality they have just passed it! Mexicans feel it more polite to give a definitive answer, even an incorrect one, than to give no answer at all, or admit they don't know. Their justly famed courtesy and friendliness, especially towards foreigners, is of course what makes travelling in the country such a pleasure.

Mexicans simply see things differently. The earliest Mexican "maps", dating from pre-Columbian times, use a series of human footprints, rather than lines, to indicate routes between places. It is as if pre-Columbian tribes valued man himself more than visible man-made changes. The locals still know best; bus and taxi drivers are the ones to ask for up-to-date information about road conditions.

INEGI's (Instituto Nacional de Estadística, Geografía e Informática) series of 1:50,000 scale topographic maps are especially useful for trekkers, campers, and for anyone proposing to spend more than a few days in any one area. They distribute their maps from their offices in every state capital and a shop in the International Airport in Mexico City.

Available from any major book store are road atlases covering the entire country. None of the ones published to date is 100% reliable. The AAA (American Automobile Association) publishes a well-researched and regularly updated guide to Mexico, available in either English or Spanish.

So, next time you're smilingly misdirected in the opposite direction to where you should be going, just have a good laugh about it and remember it's precisely these little idiosyncracies that make Mexico such a wonderful place to explore.

• • •

Bibliography

Alba-Vega, C. (editor) *Chapala. Ecología y Planeación Regional.* El Colegio de Jalisco, Guadalajara: 1990. 192 pp. Especially chapters 4 and 6. The book has 49 interesting photographs, old and new.

Araña-Alvarez, R.M., and López-González, P. *Mexcaltitán: Crónica de su Historia.* INAH/Gobierno del Estado de Nayarit: 1989. 37 pp.

Arias-Ibarra, J.G. *Jocotepec. Historia de un Pueblo.* Guadalajara: 1988. 110 pp, including 10 old photographs.

Bárcenas, A.R. "Geohistoria de una batalla." pp. 77-82 in *Geografía,* Revista del Instituto Nacional de Estadística, Geografía e Informática. INEGI. vol 1, N° 1: 1986.

Barrett, S.C.H. "Waterweed Invasions." *Scientific American,* October, 1989. pp. 66-73. Discusses biology of water hyacinth and the kariba weed.

Bashford, G.M. *Tourist Guide to Mexico.* McGraw-Hill: 1954.

Benítez-Badillo, G. *Arboles y Flores del Ajusco.* Instituto de Ecología, Mexico DF: 1985. 183 pp. Clear colour photographs, helpful identification drawings and brief descriptions of 122 flower and tree species found on Ajusco, a hill on the edge of Mexico City. Many of these species are common in Western Mexico. A well-produced but hard-to-find guide.

Bloomfield, K. "The age and significance of the Tenango basalt, Central Mexico" in *Bulletin of Vulcanology* N° 37: 1975. pp 586-595.

Bullard, F.M. "Resumen de la historia del volcán Paricutín, Michoacán, México." Part of *Excursión A15* of the Congreso Internacional de Geología, Mexico DF: 1956.

Campbell, R. *Campbell's new revised complete guide and descriptive book of Mexico.* Chicago: 1899. 351 pp. Almost as comprehensive as its title suggests. A delightful period piece.

Carlos, B. *Tamazula de Gordiano ayer y hoy.* 1990. 342 pp. The history of Tamazula.

Clark, S. *All the Best in Mexico.* Dodd, Mead & Company, New York: 1944. 284 pp.

de Alba, Antonio. *Chapala.* Banco Industrial de Jalisco, Guadalajara: 1954. 177 pp.

Escotto-Jiménez, J. *Lago de Chapala.* Gobierno de Jalisco: 1986. 72 pp. Short, summary account of basic facts and figures about Lake Chapala's hydrological characteristics.

Flores-Diaz, J.A. *Las erupciones del Volcán de Colima.* Universidad de Guadalajara: 1987. 52 pp. A complete, concise and up to date account by one of Mexico's new generation of vulcanologists.

Ford, N.D. *Fabulous Mexico, Where Everything Costs Less.* Harian Publications, New York: 1970. Includes details of relatively obscure but interesting places well off-the-beaten-track.

Franco, R. *Calendario de festividades en Jalisco.* 1985. 2 volumes, 699 pp. A month-by-month guide to the fiestas in Jalisco with historical background to many towns and villages.

Gallina, M.P. & Sangri, L. *Las Bellezas Naturales de México.* INCAFO, Madrid, Spain: 1979. 224 pp. A magnificently illustrated book covering seven National parks and ten areas of outstanding natural beauty in the country.

Garza T. de González, S. & Tommasi de Magrelli, W. "Arqueología", one of the volumes in the *Atlas Cultural de Mexico.* SEP/INAH/Planeta, Mexico DF: 1987. 190 pp.

Gobierno de Jalisco. (various contributers) *Historia de Jalisco.* Guadalajara. 1981. Comprehensive four volume account of the history of Jalisco, beautifully illustrated and produced. Enormous bibliography. Indespensable reference work for any local historian, though unfortunately lacking a full index.

Gobierno de Jalisco. *Los Municipios de Jalisco.* Sec. de Gobernación y Gobierno del Estado de Jalisco: 1988. 837 pp.

Gobierno de Michoacán. *Los Municipios de Michoacán.* Sec. de Gobernación y Gobierno del Estado de Michoacán: 1988. 531 pp.

Gobierno de Michoacán (numerous contributors). *Historia General de Michoacán.* 1989. Well illustrated and comprehensive 4 volume history.

Gulick, H.E. *Nayarit, Mexico: A Traveler's Guidebook*. Arthur H. Clark, California: 1965. 167 pp.

Guzmán, R. "Protección e investigación al habitat de Zea diploperrenis". Universidad de Guadalajara, *Documentos científicos:* 1985. 40 pp. Describes discovery and importance of wild stands of perennial corn.

INAH (Instituto Nacional de Antropología e Historia):
Tzintzuntzan, Michoacán. 1990.
Tingambato, Michoacán. 1991.
San Felipe Los Alzati. 1992.
Eight-page pamphlets describing the archaeological sites.

Jackson, E.G. *Burros and Paintbrushes*. University of Texas Press: 1985. Jackson resided in Chapala for several years in the 1920's; this is his entertaining account of his artistic endeavours in Mexico.

Janzen, D.H. (editor). *Costa Rican Natural History*. University of Chicago Press: 1983. 816 pp. A compendium of tropical and subtropical natural history by 174 different contributors with excellent species accounts, both flora and fauna, many of them relevant to Mexico.

Kendrick, J. *The Men With Wooden Feet*. The Spanish Exploration of the Pacific Northwest. NC Press, Toronto: 1985. 168 pp.

Lazcano-Sahagún, C. *Las cavernas de Cerro Grande, Estados de Colima y Jalisco*. Universidad de Guadalajara: 1988. 144 pp. Well researched account of the first modern explorations of the extensive cave systems and landforms of Cerro Grande.

Lindley, R. *Haciendas and Economic Development*. University of Texas Press: 1983. 156 pp.

LNLJ (Laboratorio Natural Las Joyas de la Sierra de Manantlán).*Plan operativo 1989-90, Reserva de la Biósfera, Sierra de Manantlán*. Universidad de Guadalajara: 1989. 90 pp.

López-González, P. *Recorrido por la Historia de Nayarit*. INEA, Tepic, Nayarit: 1986. 226 pp.

Lumholtz, C. *Unknown Mexico*. Modern edition. Rio Grande Press, New Mexico: 1973. Two volumes, 1,026 pp. The Norwegian ethnologist's classic work on Mexican native cultures, originally published in 1902.

Mason, C. T., and Mason, P. B. *A Handbook of Mexican Roadside Flora*. The University of Arizona Press: 1987. 380 pp. Line drawings supplement excellent descriptions of more than 200 common Mexican species. Includes identification key, bibliography and complete index.

México Desconocido. Excellent monthly news-stand magazine with colour photographs describing all kinds of places in Mexico.

Monasterio, F.O. and Monasterio V.O. *Mariposa Monarca, vuelo de papel.* CIDCI, Mexico, DF: 1987. 62 pp. Attractively presented description of Monarch butterflies, written for children.

Norman, J. *Terry's Guide to Mexico.* Doubleday & Company, New York: 1972. 833 pp. First published in 1909, this guide, encyclopaedic and thoroughly good reading, covers much ground that is hard to find elsewhere.

O'Hara, S. L. "Historic evidence of fluctuations in the level of Lake Pátzcuaro, Michoacán, México over the last 600 years." *The Geographical Journal,* March 1993. pp. 51-62. This author's research led to a reexamination of the Tarascans' relationship with their environment.

Ochoa, A. *Los insurgentes de Mezcala.* The College of Michoacán and the Michoacán State Government: 1985. 157 pp. This book assigns the Mezcala defenders their rightful place in Mexican Independence history. The main source for Chapter 2.

Palafox, R. A. (coordinator). *Transformaciones Mayores el en Occidente de México.* Universidad de Guadalajara: 1994. 305 pp.

Paré, L. *Los pescadores de Chapala y la defensa de su lago.* ITESO, Guadalajara: 1989. 143 pp. Detailed, well written account of the physical and economic challenges faced by Lake Chapala fishermen. Excellent bibliography.

Perry, R. *Blue Lakes and Silver Cities. Exploring Colonial West Mexico.* Espadaña Press, Santa Barbara. (in press) The definitive account of early colonial religious architecture remaining in western Mexico.

Peters, H. *La salud, la belleza y la perpetua juventud en el balneario misterioso de los Emperadores Tarascos.* 1950. 23 pp. Privately printed.

Peterson, R.T., & Chalif, E.L. *A Field Guide to Mexican Birds.* Houghton Mifflin Co. USA: 1973. 298 pp. The classic guide to Mexican birds though species also common in the US are not illustrated in the colour plates. The Spanish version, *Aves de México. Guía de Campo,* same authors, published by Editorial Diana, Mexico City, 1989, does illustrate all birds in Mexico in its 474 pages but many of the Spanish bird names quoted are not in common use in Mexico.

Piña-Chan, R. *Exploraciones Arqueológicas en Tingambato, Michoacán.* INAH, Mexico DF: 1982. 103 pp. One of the country's foremost research archaeologists explains his excavations at Tinganio.

Reyes, J.C. "Cuyutlán: Una Laguna con historia" in *Estudios Jaliscienses* N° 2, Nov. 1990. Beautifully written account of the history of the salt industry of Cuyutlán, the main source for Chapter 26.

Rulfo, J. *The Burning Plain and Other Stories*. University of Texas: 1967. 174 pp. Translated by G.D. Schade.

Rzedowski, J. *Vegetación de México*. Limusa, Mexico D.F. 1978. 432 pp. Excellent general introduction to a vast subject.

Rzedowski, J. & Equihua, M. *Atlas Cultural de Mexico. Flora*. INAH, SEP & Editorial Planeta, Mexico DF: 1987. 223 pp. Brief descriptions and colour photos of 621 species of Mexican flora divided by ecological zone. Inadequately indexed, but the best non-specialist Mexican flora available.

Sandoval, F. de P. *Obras, sucesos y fantasías en el lago Chapala*. Gobierno de Jalisco, Guadalajara: 1981. 77 pp. The changes wrought by engineering projects to the Lerma-Chapala-Santiago system with a healthy discussion of some of the more outrageous proposals which have been suggested.

SEP/Salvat. (Various authors). *El Arte Mexicano*. 1986. Richly illustrated authoritative 16 volume work covering every aspect of Mexican art from pre-Hispanic to contemporary times.

Stirling, M.W. "Solving the Mystery of Mexico's Great Stone Spheres", in *National Geographic*, 1969, pp. 294-300. The Piedras Bola explained.

Talavera-Salgado, F. Lago Chapala. *Turismo Residencial y Campesinado*. INAH, Mexico, DF: 1982. 163 pp. Well researched, illustrated, and critical account of the effects of the large non-Mexican community resident in the Ajijic area on land ownership. Interesting bibliography.

Todd, A.C. *The Search for Silver; Cornish Miners in Mexico 1824-1947*. Lodenek Press: 1977. 190 pp. A valuable and original contribution to research into Mexican silver production post-Independence and its links to Engand.

Toor, F. *A Treasury of Mexican Folkways*. Crown, New York: 1947. Reprinted in 1985 by Bonanza Books, New York. 566 pp. Classic but dated work on all kinds of customs and fiestas.

t'Serstevens, A. *Mexico -Three-Storeyed Land*. Hutchinson: 1959. 368 pp. English edition of work originally published in French. A highly idiosyncratic but revealing travelogue of both joys and nightmares.

Tweedie, A. *Mexico as I Saw It*. Macmillan, New York: 1901. 472 pp. A delightful account of one woman's exhaustive travels through Mexico just before the

Revolution.

UNAM/INEGI *Geología de la República Mexicana.* 1984. 88 pp.

Universidad de Guadalajara. *Lago de Chapala, investigación actualizada 1983.*
Universidad de Guadalajara, Instituto de Geografía y Estadística, Instituto
de Astronomía y Meteorológica, Guadalajara: 1983. 67 pp. Short scientific
overview of the lake, with statistical appendices covering local climate and
historic lake levels.

Urquhart, F.A. "Found at last: The Monarch's winter home". *National Geographic,*
August 1976. pp. 160-173. The first popular publication of the Monarch's
Mexican habitat, completely without location information.

Walton, N.K. "Tequila." British Chamber of Commerce Magazine, Mexico City.
1977. First published in *Américas,* magazine of the Organization of
American States.

Wright, N.P. *Mexican Kaleidoscope.* Heinemann: 1947. 175 pp.
A Mexican Medley for the Curious. Tolteca Editions, Mexico: 1961. 159
pp. Fun to read miscellanies of the many and varied aspects of the country
which appealed to this former British Military Attache and great lover of
Mexico.

Yarza de la Torre, E. *Volcanes de México.* UAEM, Mexico: 1983. 264 pp. Covers
all aspects of vulcanicity in Mexico with an extensive bibliography.

• • •

Index

• • •

The Author

G eographer and naturalist, Tony Burton, born in England in 1953, has graduate degrees from Cambridge and London Universities and is a Fellow of the Royal Geographical Society. He has lived in Mexico since 1979.

This is his second book; the first, about the West Indies, sold more than 10,000 copies. He has had numerous articles published on ecotourism, non-tourist Mexico and academic fieldwork, in both English and Spanish. He is a three-time winner of ARETUR's annual international travel-writing competition for articles about Mexico.

Since 1986 he has directed Odisea México, a non-profit organization promoting sound scientific methods of environmental education for every age-group. He also organises and leads a limited number of ecotourist excursions open to the general public each year.

The Illustrator

M ark Eager, born in Canada in 1959, inherited artistic talents which have run in his family for generations. He has lived in Mexico since 1975 and finished his schooling in Guadalajara. He was co-proprietor for many years of "The Tequila Tree", the well-known Mexican art and handicrafts store in Vancouver, Canada. A keen interest in Mexican architecture and design has taken him throughout the country.

He and his Mexican wife, Martha, live in Ajijic. This is the first book he has illustrated.

• • •